An Outdated Gospel

The Setting of the Cross in the West

Rene Caza

WestBow
PRESS
A DIVISION OF THOMAS NELSON

Copyright © 2010 Rene Caza

All rights reserved. No part of this book may be used or reproduced by any means, graphic, electronic, or mechanical, including photocopying, recording, taping or by any information storage retrieval system without the written permission of the publisher except in the case of brief quotations embodied in critical articles and reviews.

WestBow Press books may be ordered through booksellers or by contacting:

WestBow Press
A Division of Thomas Nelson
1663 Liberty Drive
Bloomington, IN 47403
www.westbowpress.com
1-(866) 928-1240

Because of the dynamic nature of the Internet, any Web addresses or links contained in this book may have changed since publication and may no longer be valid. The views expressed in this work are solely those of the author and do not necessarily reflect the views of the publisher, and the publisher hereby disclaims any responsibility for them.

Any people depicted in stock imagery provided by Thinkstock are models, and such images are being used for illustrative purposes only.

Certain stock imagery © Thinkstock.

Bible quotes taken from New American Standard
Bible unless otherwise stated in the text.

ISBN: 978-1-4497-0961-7 (sc)
ISBN: 978-1-4497-0960-0 (dj)
ISBN: 978-1-4497-0959-4 (e)

Library of Congress Control Number: 2010941854

Printed in the United States of America

WestBow Press rev. date: 12/30/2010

Contents

Acknowledgements		vii
Foreword by Rev. Gerrie Armaly		ix
Preface		xi
1	Error Smuggled In	1
2	The Antique Cross	12
3	Nevertheless Not My Will	26
4	What About Me	39
5	Gateway to an Open Heaven	56
6	Pressed Into Conformity	62
7	I Did It My Way	79
8	On the Desert Floor	91
9	Testing 101	105
10	Temptation 101	121
11	Honestly, Where Are We Going?	135
12	The Offense of the Cross	151
13	Gethsemane	162
Author Biography		169

Acknowledgements

Special thanks to my son Daniel for all the technical help and who patiently worked through the editing and original cover design. To my wife Yvonne whose support and 'space' allowed me to work uninterrupted, and Stephanie my daughter who helped me by trying to locate 'saved' but lost files.

Most importantly I want to thank my Heavenly Father for His love, grace and affirmation who walked through with me and kept me at His side in some very dark times, and for guiding me through this work .

Foreword
by Rev. Gerrie Armaly

"God forbid that I should glory in anything but the cross...." A book for all of us, *The Setting of the Cross in the West* takes a hard look at the current state of the church in North America. Have we left behind the timeless truth of "clinging to the old rugged Cross"? With the feel good gospel that North America has embraced, much of the church no longer understands the inner workings of the Cross – the necessity of dying to self and embracing the cross in order to move into an intimate relationship with our Saviour, Jesus Christ. The Cross that saved us is also the Cross that forms us!

Rene, a teacher in the church, has dug into the word of God with great concern as he has watched unsettling changes in the Body of Christ over the last two decades. A great alarm resounds throughout the pages of this book for the church to wake up and understand that the discipline of the Cross and dying to self are the only ways to become mature sons and daughters of the Father.

What has happened to this concept in North America? Why has the church abandoned the teachings of the early church: that to overcome in tribulations and to rejoice in trials that are allowed to come into our lives forms the character of Christ in us? Paul states in Romans 5:3 that we must glory in tribulations, knowing that tribulation produces perseverance; and perseverance, character; and character, hope. This book takes a thorough look at these often passed over scriptures.

Rene, like all of us, has experienced many difficulties in life, but these difficulties have caused him to press into the Lord and His Word to get his answers and to grow in grace. As his pastor, I have watched him seek the face of God for the strength to mature and worship in trials and hardships.

This book presents deep and compelling truths that were once commonplace in everyday Christianity, but now seem foreign and mysterious to much of the church. Truth rings clear throughout this book; we must become "partakers in the fellowship of His sufferings" to become mature sons and daughters. I encourage you to pray as you read so that you too can embrace "the old rugged Cross" and become all that Christ has destined you to be for the sake of His Kingdom.

Dr. Gerrie Armaly
Senior Pastor and Founder of
Antioch Christian Ministries

Preface

What book can begin to completely grasp and explain the far-reaching work Jesus Christ accomplished on the cross? Each new insight and revelation we have about the cross brings us more understanding of its various aspects clearly depicted in Scripture. As I have continued to be taught and disciplined in the 'ways' of the cross, a deeper personal relationship with my Father has opened up to me. These 'ways' have also, although painfully at times, reared me into a more balanced and mature disciple and son.

In this study, I have endeavored to present a fresh look at what I would term the 'work of the cross in the human heart' rather than deal with the many new and emerging teachings that seems to strengthen our natural man instead of crucifying it. Concentrating on the beauty and wisdom that God intended as the result of our applying the cross to our own lives would be time and energy, I believe, better spent.

The growing focus on the gifts of the spirit, on the manifold anointings, conference after conference intent on tapping into the power of God – these, to name a few, have captured center stage placing greater significance on 'how to' receive from God. I am certainly not discounting the importance of these gifts and abilities, but where is the balance? One look at the overall state of the North American Christian church reveals, in my opinion, a very carnal and shallow Christianity. We have become a consumer driven 'organism';

our resemblance to the Corinthian church is uncanny. The believers in Corinth, though they did not lack in any gift, were still carnal, fleshy and unable to digest solid food (1 Cor.1:7; 3:3).

The cross that saved us is the same cross that conforms us into the image of Jesus Christ. Our salvation through the shed blood and sacrifice of Jesus on the cross opened the entrance into His eternal kingdom. However this is just the beginning. The cross that represents death is the cross that beckons us to lay our will aside to follow Christ into the wilderness so that we might become a "partaker in the fellowship of His sufferings."

Spiritual infancy like its natural counterpart is all around us – a very self-serving mindset indeed. We have wrongly concluded that Christ-likeness is associated only with doing His works without actually learning His 'ways'. A true passage into spiritual adulthood is marked by a passionate desire to embrace the cross, echoing the words of Jesus himself: "I delight to do Thy will O my God; Thy law is written in my heart" (Ps. 40:8).

The discipline of the cross is the threshold of our becoming 'mature sons and daughters' of God: no longer laborers in the vineyards crying out 'give me, give me', but Sons awakened to their inheritance pleading with the Father 'please make me.'

Our quest as healthy, maturing believers should mirror the passage in 1 John 2:6 "The one who says he abides in Him, ought himself to walk in the same manner as He walked."

In reading these chapters, you will notice a repetition of the central theme of this book. My intent has been to weave this topic throughout like a mosaic of sorts. There is a tapestry laid out, scripturally displaying the same basic unshakeable truth: If we will reign with Him, we must also suffer for Him (2 Timothy 2:12). The reiteration is further intended to anchor the paramount teaching of the cross deep into our understanding while illustrating the divine strategy to spiritual maturity. Simply put, this strategy involves the conforming aspects of decimating the natural man by means of suffering adversity, misunderstanding, agony, isolation, barrenness and failure.

I make no apologies for what I believe scripture clearly teaches on 'the fellowship of His sufferings'. Although, it may be difficult to embrace one's own cross in a church world of 'self-ism' (if I may coin a phrase), it is essential for the Church and each disciple to once again reacquaint themselves with this subject (through renewed study) and let the word of God speak for itself. The volume of material referencing the cross is so overwhelming that it may astonish you.

Any teaching on victory over sin or doctrine of sanctification is incomplete if it does not address the 'strength' of our natural man. God must take hold of each disciple to reveal and subdue the natural source of his or her strength. This is considered by some to be the negative side of the Gospel. However, this attitude does not negate the fact that, quite often, before one can build - in this case the true character of Christ - a great deal of demolition is necessary. The former self-serving, self-absorbed 'structure' must give way to a new formation, a holy edifice: the House of the Lord established in the heart of a mature 'son'. (The term 'son' is used in a general sense to describe both male and female).

We, His unique creations are waiting anxiously for the revealing of our 'son-ship', and the vehicle that will bring that about and remove our illegitimacy will be the loving discipline of the Lord (Hebrews 12:8). Let us not regard lightly the discipline of the Lord, nor faint when correction comes our way, for those whom the Lord loves He disciplines and scourges every Son whom He receives (Hebrews 12:5-6). We are exhorted by Peter to follow in the same steps as Jesus. Since Jesus suffered in the flesh, we are to arm or equip ourselves with the same mindset.

Our walk is a matter of choices. We have already made the choice to follow Jesus Christ. Now other choices face us that will determine the measure of authority and influence that will be entrusted to us in His Kingdom on this earth. These are not choices between Heaven and Hell since this has already been settled when we accepted Christ, but the choices we make from that point on, day by day, will reveal how much free access we have truly given the Lord to enter into our 'inner sanctuary'. Here in this well protected and secure place our shared love for Jesus Christ will allow the Lord to lovingly but firmly heal and transform our thoughts, attitudes, mindsets, including areas that have been deeply entrenched, wounded, shattered and broken, places we would never choose to visit again or allow anyone else to approach.

At this juncture in our 'crisis' moments Christ will be able to whisper peace into our turmoil and pain as He enters in and begins to arrange our lives in 'right order'. It is time that the children of the Kingdom embrace the cross and press into their inheritance as full grown sons of God.

"God gives us the cross and the cross gives us God"
Madame Guyon

Chapter 1

Error Smuggled In

Imagine for a moment a large building with a security system. All the monitors, cameras and motion sensors are in place. The doors are locked. But surprisingly, we discover that an unauthorized entry has occurred; someone has entered the building undetected and is now in the process of stealing and vandalizing its contents. The security of the building has been compromised and now all of the occupants are at risk.

The church in the West is this building and this is by no means an overstatement. In fact, if it were possible and one could review and scrutinize the church's security tapes over the last few decades we would be shocked to see how much damage has been done and continues to be done by these, now resident, intruders. The most alarming fact is that little has been done to correct the situation. The security system has not been improved, no alarms have been sounded and no one has been held accountable for the damage. The problem continues.

We've all seen enough movies to understand that places of great importance have great security. The security should at least be adequate enough to protect the contents. Anything of value has to be protected and kept safe: this is just common sense. Valuables are always in danger of falling within the crosshairs of those who would gladly dispossess us of them.

> The church in the West has been compromised in the sense that it has been infiltrated by teachers and teaching that have removed, obscured and replaced some of the most precious possessions it has - its foundational truth and teachings. However, few seem to be aware that this 'slight of hand' has occurred! In the original's place rests a counterfeit, a counterfeit that has gone undetected. This substitute is flourishing unhindered at an alarming pace and we will realize one day, at an awful price.

We have had a number of thefts in the church over its long history, only to have the truth restored centuries later. A case in point would be Martin Luther's "justification by faith" doctrine. But eventually, faith was removed and replaced with a works doctrine that slid the church into one of the darkest chapters in its history. From its very birth the church has been vigilant to defend and contend for "the faith", yet there have been perilous times where the light seemed to go out, but fortunately, was never fully extinguished.

Another article of faith restored is the foundational aspects of the priesthood of the believer. The awesome calling and setting apart of each person as a priest unto God had been stripped away and replaced by a special, privileged class of learned men called clergy. These men, by human appointment, were to represent the laity: a spiritually underprivileged class of domestic, manual workers – in other words everybody else. They were considered unqualified to approach a Holy God and enjoy a personal relationship with Him. They were denied access to the Bible's liberating truth and left to accept the dictates of craftily thought out doctrines, which in some circles continues to this day.

We could go on to enumerate the teaching of the Holy Spirit, the baptism, the infilling, the endued power in the believer's life by the Holy Spirit, the restoring of the five-fold offices to the Church: the apostle, the prophet, the evangelist, pastor and teacher.

These gifts and enablements are given to the body by the ascended Christ and by the workings of the Holy Spirit. However different their varieties and functions, it is the same God who works all things in all people. Some of these are received with open arms while others are still rejected. Yet they are nonetheless scriptural and relevant for the Church of Jesus Christ today. Biblically sound and clearly taught in scripture, they are not intended only for a certain dispensation of time but until we all "attain to the unity of the faith, and of the knowledge of the Son of God, to a mature man, to the measure of the stature which belongs to the fullness of Christ" (Ephesians 4: 13; 1 Corinthians 12: 1- 14). All of which I believe we have not attained.

> Men of every age, pawns themselves in a war for their hearts, minds and ultimately their eternal souls have wreaked havoc on the Church, attempting to squash it either with physical powers, made up of armies and emperors, or with insidious and crafty doctrines that have crept in undetected. These, in time, resulted in splits and factions further distorting the truth and maligning the names and characters of those who have labored so hard in establishing the foundations and structure of the Church. Even to the point of denying Jesus Himself who saved them. (Read 2 Peter 2: 1-3)

We read in Jude 1:3, "Beloved while I was making every effort to write to you about our common salvation, I felt the necessity to write to you appealing that you contend earnestly for the faith which was once for all handed down to the saints" (NASB).

One may not immediately discern the urgency of this verse or grasp the scope of the spiritual war which had already engulfed the Church. Certain people had stealthily brought error into the early Church. One gets the sense that Jude is sounding an alarm as he details the present condition of the church. He is appealing to all those "called beloved in God the Father and kept for Jesus Christ" (1:1).

What is the appeal? To contend earnestly for the faith or put another way 'to struggle and fight for the faith that was delivered or yielded to the saints'. This appeal was not some unfounded "Cry wolf": the wolves were already in the barn!

Starting at verse 4 we read, "For certain persons have crept in unnoticed, those who were long beforehand marked out for this condemnation, ungodly persons who turn the grace of our Lord into licentiousness and deny our only Master and Lord Jesus Christ." This verse illuminates their threatening motive. The reason why these men "crept" in, or in the Greek rendering, 'moved in stealthily, alongside' the believers in the Church, was to pervert the true grace of God into a license to live in a continued state of lawlessness, immorality and wantonness while enjoying the benefits of the Christian community.

> They could have remained in the world and lived their lives of wantonness and lust without reproof. So why become part of the Body and risk condemnation and rejection from that Body for an apparent void or lack of repentance and godly fruit? Unless of course it was a deceptive strategy with the hope to spread heresy that everyone, or many would eventually buy into. You could say this was the original prototype of "cheap grace."

Dietrich Bonheoffer in his book, "The Cost of Discipleship," describes "cheap grace" as "the preaching of forgiveness without repentance, baptism without church discipline, communion without confession. Cheap grace is grace without discipleship, grace without the cross, grace without Jesus Christ, living and incarnate."(page 47)

This is a grace which places no requirements on the believer. Yes, grace needs to be preached in such liberal and generous terms that we may need to ask ourselves "does this grace even allow me to sin?"

The answer is, no, of course not, but it makes allowance for sin. As deep, as large and as often as we fail, grace is not rendered deficient by our great need of it. "…but where sin increased, grace abounded all the more…" (Romans 5:20). There is a liberty and freedom in a true grace teaching that baffles the legalist. We are able to live and breathe without a hundred and one parameters chaining us to some invisible stake in the ground called conformity to the group, sect or denomination.

The proponents of this perverse grace were seeking a license to continue in their old sinful habits. They desired forgiveness for their sin but were unwilling to repent of their ways and attitudes thus stopping short of forgiveness of the sinner because they did not truly desire it. They wanted to continue in their sinful ways and spread this counterfeit grace message as genuine - no repentance, no confession, no cross.

Denying our Lord and Master is a heavy charge against anyone and Jude lays down the line. That someone would knowingly deny the Lord, having been genuinely born again, having seen and tasted the goodness of God, and then turn around and deny Him and even work against Him is disturbing. However disturbing, it is indeed possible. The type of denial that Jude is referring to in this verse is a simple one: it is a denial that contradicts the very essence and purpose of God's grace through the saving work of Jesus Christ. To deny His work is in my opinion to deny the Lord Himself.

The Pharisees of Jesus day were a prime example of this. Unwilling to acknowledge the many miracles He performed as being from God, they blatantly accused Him of doing so by the power of the devil.

Notice that the scripture in verse 4 says "ungodly persons." Now were they heathen, ungodly persons that crept in unaware? This is possible but highly unlikely. Strange people coming into your fellowship would raise a few eyebrows, especially if they started promoting doctrines that were odd and unfamiliar. But if a person had been around for a period of time, say a member of the church, and they had earned a measure of respect and spiritual stature then the possibility of them advancing their revelation or new teaching is much greater. In this way, the 'new doctrine' has a much greater chance of being rooted and established than any effort from some ungodly stranger in our midst.

However, if these same people hold a position of authority and teach their congregations, there is little to inhibit the error from taking root in their assemblies. 2 Peter 2:1 teaches "But false prophets also arose among the people, just as there will also be among you, who will secretly introduce destructive heresies, even denying the Master who bought them, bringing swift destruction upon themselves" (NASB).

> We certainly take note of the fact that these were false prophets. But more startling is the phrase "arose among the people." They were not strangers creeping in rather these "false prophets" came from among them and were undetected because they had already gained trust and confidence among the body of believers. At some point, these teachings were spawned in hope to germinate in the hearts and minds of believers. Why would a believer do that, or better yet, could a believer intentionally bring forth what the Bible labels "destructive or damnable heresies"?

The short answer at this point would be yes, for the same reason that Judas betrayed Jesus or Demas abandoned Paul. One's personal motivation may never come to the light of day and people are still free to make their own choices, right or wrong.

Remember the analogy at the beginning of this chapter about the building and its security system. The building was compromised and yet no intruder was detected. The only obvious conclusion would be to assume, with some accuracy, that there was someone in the building who was "cleared" to be in the building that really should not have been allowed to be in the building.

2 Peter 2:1 reveals the strategy of these characters. These false teachers will "secretly introduce destructive heresies" as the King

James reads: "there shall be false teachers among you who privily (privately) shall bring in damnable heresies."

The Greek here is of great value in understanding this verse: "privily shall bring in." The Greek word here is *'paraeisago'* which is a compound word made up of three words:
- **para**: 'alongside and very close' from which we get our word parasite. It doesn't get much closer than that!
- **eis**: means 'into' and conveys the idea of penetration.
- **ago**: simply put means 'I lead'.

Let us take these three words and put them together in the context of what Peter is teaching here. Basically, he is saying: These false teachers are leading the way into our minds and bringing in destructive heresies alongside of the truth to avoid detection and to penetrate the minds of the hearers. False teaching has to be intertwined with truth to get in 'undetected' and it will be taught to the Church by those already in the Church. You might say it is being smuggled in.

The responsibility of the Church is to continue to be vigilant, not necessarily posting sentries at the front door for Sunday service or the weekly Bible study, but monitoring the teaching we hear day to day or week to week. Some disputes may not be worth the energy to contend for because many just fizzle out on their own, but there are some teachings that necessitate we be as astute as the Berean Christians.

The Bereans were more noble minded than the Christians of Thessalonica "for they received the word with great eagerness, examining the scriptures daily to see if these things were so" (Acts 17: 10, 11 NASB).

> The 'absence' of certain foundational truth taught and passed down to us for the life and well being of the Body provides fertile ground for other strange teaching to take hold and flourish. Foundational truth has to be guarded from all counterfeits.

Every believer has to take some serious spiritual inventory on a regular base. We need to ask ourselves periodically; does what I believe produce godly fruit in my life? Are these teachings in line with Biblical truth and not just our own particular Church doctrines? To love the truth we may have to go outside the camp of familiarity and our own denominational indoctrination we automatically accept at times without question.

Paul, the apostle, dealt with a number of false teachings and counterfeit doctrines. There were the Gnostics - the 'I know people' - with all their 'super spiritual' revelations and visions that were above scriptural scrutiny. Then there were Judaizers who constantly were looking for inroads with their brand of legalism and control trying to reintroduce the new believers into an old bondage. Then there was also Hymenaeus and Philetus who went around teaching that the resurrection of the dead had already taken place, with a host of others trying to merchandize their doctrinal wares and erroneous teachings.

Note in 2 Timothy 2:18: "men who have gone astray from the truth" or men who once knew and chose a contrary doctrine for whatever reason and were now teaching error yet still believing it to be the truth.

All of us at some point whether we want to admit it or not have embraced and may have even taught error or what may have become a heresy. The point being, anyone can at some point be deceived with some form of teaching, and even be a conduit of some scriptural inaccuracy. However, when the truth came "knocking on our door", how did we receive the correction?

The simple fact remains: many times we believe what we choose to believe and are convinced that it is the truth even if it is not. Therefore it is crucial that we walk in humility and remain teachable especially if we achieve fame or great success in life. In fact, as we have seen in times past the bigger the name the more isolated and insulated famous or successful personalities become towards any course adjustments or correction. Their mindset being, 'whom do I submit to, I am renowned in the land'? Everyone is envious of my ministry,' and so any form of counsel may be viewed as criticism and is dismissed or marginalized.

I will return to the building (church) analogy. If we are all occupants of the same building, actually let's take it further, if we are all family (God's family?) should not our main interest be solely for the safety and security of our fellow occupants, providing the utmost security for what has been entrusted to us by the owner God? Unfortunately the history of the church says otherwise. Church history is replete with episodes of one faction erecting walls within 'the building' to isolate themselves from other groups, or to isolate other 'occupants'. Time after time, communication lines were strained and then cut off. Any warnings or alarms did little to correct overall problems in the building and each group was content to monitor, to varying degrees, their own doorways. While some were more vigilant to contend for the overall security of the building, others seemed only focused on their own interest.

Church history bears witness that certain interpretations of scripture divided the church which led to denominational walls that further isolated the Body of Christ. Each denomination embraced their particular brand or view all the while raising the bar of performance requiring their disciples to follow more exclusive stringent demands. Other groups decried the errors infiltrating the early church and genuinely tried to stop the influx that threatened to undermine the understood true scriptural teaching of the day.

I realize this is a simplistic overall view of what we have evolved into as the church in the West. Yet I think it gets the point across that we are no longer unified on a large scale as one body of believers entrusted with treasure given to us by the Lord Himself. Many who seek their own interest would like nothing more than to steal, kill and destroy the teachings (treasures) and even the Lord Himself if they could. Those inside the 'building' who are, for whatever personal reasons of gain, choosing to advance their own agendas and forgetting what has been entrusted to them by the Lord will one day stand before the Lord. There we will all give an account of what we have said and done in respect to "dividing accurately the word of truth" in the name of God.

> Can we afford to disregard the past and continue to stand by and watch as other great tenets of the faith are either hi-jacked or disregarded altogether as the church moves towards another Dark Age: one that is rooted and misguided with the exaltation of self interest, self serving, self love; a Gospel that caters to every whim of our carnal man; a message that is cloaked to appeal to our carnal man yet lacks the transforming power of the Cross to transform the man?

I would like to interject a comment here that I will cover more extensively in a later chapter. There is an increasing surge of desire in the Church for power and miracles. This is certainly scriptural in the sense of wanting to see God's Spirit moving through the church as the gospel is preached with signs following, but alarming on the other hand if it is generated by human zeal and energy. It is frightening if it is a spiritual form of manipulation being exercised over groups of desperate believers wanting nothing more than to be used by God to perform signs and wonders. The point being: power in the hands of anyone with ulterior motives is dangerous. The natural man within must be dealt with by the cross, a person cannot allow ambition and desire to marginalize the Holy Spirit, and yet that is exactly what is happening as the church puts forward its seeker friendly appeals with a generic Gospel that cannot convict anyone of sin.

> Any teaching that leaves the flesh intact and uncrucified where man can remain unbroken, strong in himself and where his natural skills and abilities point back towards himself only to edify himself, is evidence enough that the Cross has not been applied or allowed to carry on its deadly but life transforming process.

The Bible teaches "the mind set on the flesh is hostile towards God, for it does not subject itself to the law of God for it is not even able to do so" (Rom. 8:7 NASB). Left to our own natural thinking, our carnal minds can only produce thoughts that are sinful, self-serving and hostile towards God. In fact, our carnal minds CANNOT subject or submit themselves to God; only as we choose to be led by the Spirit of God can we actually begin to think spiritual thoughts that please the Lord.

Chapter 2

The Antique Cross

The Cross and its teachings have largely been relegated to the attic as one would store an antique or some other old piece of furniture. Although it may hold some personal sentiment and memories, it no longer has any real place on the main floor.

In light of what is being generated in the area of new teaching, what speaks the loudest as to its absence in these 'novel' teachings is the shear lack of any emphasis on the Cross. This is in essence what Jesus taught in Mathew 10:38-39: "and he who does not take up his cross and follow Me is not worthy of Me. He who has found his life will lose it, and he who has lost his life for My sake will find it." All Christians who want to walk in the abundant life of the Spirit will find out soon enough that there are no shortcuts to spiritual maturity or intimacy with their heavenly Father.

The Master himself, Jesus Christ, has called us all as His disciples to "come and take up our cross and follow [Him]" (Mathew 10:38). The 'loss of our life' is not a one time, one moment decision. Rather it will be, if we want to become the fully mature Sons that God is calling us to be, an ongoing moment-by-moment, situational choice, circumstance choice, an ethical choice and a character choice. "[We]", as John the Baptist so rightly put it, "must decrease and He (Jesus) must increase" (John 3:30).

> Dying to self is the normal Christian lifestyle - period! We are not to be surprised or think it strange when we experience, as the King James reads, "fiery trials which [are] to try you...: But rejoice inasmuch as ye are partakers of Christ's sufferings..." (1 Peter 4:12-13).

Someone once said, "The Cross has not lost its power only its appeal." Between the worlds's narcissistic spirit of self-love and the extreme unbalanced teaching of the church - which in many cases is the very reflection of the world's spirit - a very selfish, self-centered gospel lives on. Is it any wonder when we look at statistics on abortion and divorce that we see no great differences when we should contrast with the world as night does with day?

What about the homosexual issue? Whole denominations are caving in to the "spirit of this age" which should be of no surprise to anyone since this spirit has found much ground in the modern day believer's heart and mind. It has constructed every manner of argument to advance its liberalistic, lusts-of-the-flesh agenda under the guise of being broad minded and liberated from the 'old standards'.

We have ceased to call a "spade a spade" or sin a sin. There is a mounting pressure from both the spiritual world and the natural - the natural being the instrument in the hand of demonic spiritual influences flexing its muscle, effectively conforming the believer into the pattern of this age and we can no longer discern the compromise!

However, there is no power on the planet that can "take down" the church. In its D.N.A. resides all the power of the resurrection. "His divine power has granted to us all things that pertain to life and godliness" but we may have forgotten that this power comes through "the true knowledge of Him who called us by His own glory and excellence (2 Peter1:3). Each individual believer, being part of a larger body of believers, must, as Jude appealed, "contend earnestly for the faith which was once for all delivered to the saints" (Jude 3).

The primary focus of this book is to look, with a fresh perspective, at the beauty of the cross of Christ, the eternal wisdom of God in the cross and the eternal purpose of God to transform each believer from babes to mature sons and daughters of God: this can ONLY be done through the cross of Christ.

The power and revival that the Church so longs for is not found in some new teaching but rather in 'dying to self' - some very old teaching. The very core of revival is to bring back to life that which is dead or dying. This was our condition when Jesus Christ entered our lives and brought us to life. This however is not the central theme the church should be pursuing; we more than likely need to experience an ongoing death to self that we might come into more of His life.

Revival means to revive something that is dead. The church was never meant to be dead. The church was so equipped to live, grow and reproduce itself as it embraced the life-giving power of the Cross and the enduring resurrection life found in dying daily yet living abundantly at the same time (2 Cor. 4:10-16).

Revival is an event, yes, and a divine event as God in His sovereignty steps in to revitalize and awaken a church, a community, even a nation. It may lasts for a few days, weeks or even years but it does end. However, this should not be the mainstay of the church. We thank God for His extraordinary visitation and would like nothing more if He hung around in like fashion on a permanent basis. But if we are doing what He told us to do and are working alongside His Holy Spirit then we have to agree with the scripture that teaches us "He has given us all things that pertain to life and godliness through the knowledge of Him…" (2 Peter 1:3). God alone will decide who and when another great move will be needed. "All things" means "all things" and it is found in the true knowing of Him and the countless aspects of His nature and character.

However, the status quo we are experiencing is certainly not all that God has intended for us to walk in. The reality may be that God entrusts a certain expression of His body with miraculous signs and wonders only to watch the rest of us all rise up with envy and strife between ourselves.

The life of a disciple is a life of submission to the Lordship of Christ and the road He chooses for each one who names His name will be marked with varying degrees of suffering. It's just par for the course. An ongoing 'revival' erupts in the heart of that individual disciple who lays down his life and follows Jesus. Imagine what a church full of similar disciples would look like on a daily basis year after year. Do you not think their communities would be affected, even their nation?

Are our revivals marked only with shouts, dancing, and some healings? What about an ongoing fervent love for Christ and His people? What about rolling up our sleeves and getting to work serving people in some very basic and practical ways and not idly waiting for goose bumps or other manifestations. God just might approve of our loving His body enough to serve in our local churches or communities.

> The moral decay of a nation is not a sign in and of itself that God is about to move in a particular way. The church has to maintain a clear focus on Christ alone. The Holy Spirit was given to the church to lead, guide and empower it to overcome all obstacles and to teach it into all aspects of godliness. Revival can never take the place of the Holy Spirit, revival is not the 'be all to end all' of our issues. One look over church history reveals the sad fact that revival was sandwiched in between the decadent condition before and was followed by a similar condition afterwards.

Could it be possible that God may send persecution or a depression to re ignite the church and awaken it out of its passive state? No, let us not despise any God ordained season where the church is laid low or is wandering in a desert place of God's appointment. Like in the

'Book of Acts' a Saul arose and began to persecute and kill believers which sent the saints and the message outward in every direction.

God may be in the process of removing every object, structure and person we may have come to put our trust in, for the purpose that He would have us all to Himself without any rivals to divert His praise or credit.

The visitation I believe Jesus spoke about was an ongoing revelation of Him. A revelation of His mercy, grace and love that would continue to generate gratitude, worship and awe in every believer intent on following Him no matter where He leads. We need more than an event or a lightning bolt of God's magnificent power on display however great and wonderful that may be.

The church needs to return a place of brokenness, repentance and humility, then, and maybe only then, as we present ourselves as living sacrifices the fire that was ignited at Pentecost will be rekindled afresh in us and the wind of the Holy Ghost will engulf the western church for generations to come. May this be our goal, our prayer and our destiny.

There is a slow but methodical strategy that whispers we leave aside some of the most basic yet transforming truths in scripture and introduce a hybrid of sorts in their place. This is not new but repackaged false teaching that exalts creation and man above his Creator. This is not to say that God is right out of the picture, no, that would be too obvious. Rather, God is brought across more like a good old friend of the family. You know the kind that is not very relevant today. We allow Him into our conversation but no one really puts much stock in His words. Why? Because there is so much 'new enlightenment' to take in and His words are no longer pertinent or to be taken literally or as absolute truth.

Our point of reference has shifted: God's word is no longer the benchmark by which we align all other buildings and future construction. We have accepted new standards, other standards, strange standards. We now have multiple reference points that carry as much importance as the Bible, which in time, if not corrected will be our undoing.

> Each generation of Christians has had to lift up the Cross of Christ. In each generation, many enemies of the Cross have risen up to try to discredit its testimony, its power and beauty. The Cross has been derided as outdated, called violent and bloody - a horrible blemish on our history. We have always been faced with spiritual assaults against the truth; they are part and parcel of our walk but what we see happening in our generation with the emergence of so many alternative truths is alarming. This can only be described as an all out spiritual invasion through the media with the intent to shift the minds and attitudes of believers and to influence this younger generation coming up to abandon the 'old ways'.

This is as good a place as any to say that if the church passes on only information to this next generation we will be abandoning them to the world, their flesh and lastly the devil. We keep hearing that the next generation that is so gifted bright and full of potential will be used of God to sweep the nations with a revival full of the glory of God. Certainly, that would be awesome. However, do we think that this younger generation is somewhat more divine than the previous and that they are devoid of a carnal nature?

Without the foundation of the cross in place and the understanding that they are totally dependant on a God who provides them all manner of grace, mercy and authority, can we expect that they will turn out any different then the rest of us who have run aground on our own steam and human potential.

When the trial comes (and they will come), will they fall away and return to a life with less conflict? Will a younger generation be able to discern and embrace a God who allows them and even plans a wilderness trek for them to undue the various aspects of their carnal natures? Are we teaching them how God Himself will demand that their lives, dreams and aspirations be surrendered at the cross before a holy God who will bless and multiply His sacrifice as Abraham surrendered Isaac up in sacrifice? This hope we have for our younger people will be de-railed not far from the station if they are sent out only on hype, some gifting and a teaching that they are to bring revival to the land.

The standard must be kept in place! Let us teach them thoroughly on the 'ways' of God; let us prepare them for heartache and failure and that, yes, things can go terribly wrong even for Christians. Let us be willing to break with the popular teachings of this day and age and return to the Antique Cross.

> There is a slow methodical stepping away from the faith, an embracing of other strange teaching and an attitude that is passive towards the principles of denying self. These are all indicators, undetectable mind shifts, which in turn open the door to unbridled strong desire for the things of this world, but this hardly raises an eyebrow anymore. We are certainly in the latter times.

A very interesting and timely verse in 1 Timothy 4:1 reads "Now the Spirit speaketh expressly that in the latter times some shall depart from the faith, giving heed to seducing spirits, and doctrines of devils…"(KJV).

Let us break this verse down by individual words and look at their original Greek meaning.
- "Now the Spirit speaketh expressly": Expressly (*rhetos* gr.) means clearly, vividly unmistakable, undeniable, and definite.
- "That in the latter": Latter (*husteros* gr.) means the extreme end of something, very last season or period of time, the very end of something.
- "Times some shall depart": Depart (*aphistemi* gr.), two words: 1- to stand, 2- away. We could say 'to stand away or step away or withdraw from'. This word is the same word we derive the word "apostate" - from the faith.

Let us put the thoughts rendered here in sentence form: 'Now the Spirit speaketh clearly, vividly and undeniably that in the very last season, the extreme end of time some shall step away, actually they will withdraw from the faith.'

Now the scripture does not say they will 'reject' the faith but rather that they will 'step away' from it or withdraw from it. To reject the faith is a deliberate and intentional decision. This verse suggests that this withdrawal will be a slow unintentional act, a very subtle process taking place at the end of the age.

The second part of the verse reads "giving heed to seducing spirits and doctrines of devils...."Let us take a closer look at the last segment of verse 1.

- "giving heed" (*prosecho* gr.): to turn one's mind to or giving oneself up to.
- "seducing spirits"(*planos* gr.): an adjective signifying wandering or leading astray, seducing; as a noun , it denotes an imposter of the vagabond type, any kind of deceiver or corrupter.
- "doctrines" (*disdaskalia* gr.): that which is taught, doctrine, teaching, instruction.
- "of devils." (*daimonion* gr.) devil, god, a deity.

Let's put this verse back together with a more amplified rendering. Verse 1: 'Now the Spirit speaketh clearly, vividly and undeniably that in the very last season - the extreme end of time - some will step away, actually they will withdraw from the faith, giving heed as they turn their minds over to deceiving, corrupt spirits posing as the real thing which are giving instruction, teaching so called doctrines but are actually demonic teachings with the purpose of deceiving the hearers.'

Reality dictates that this will not be a demon standing up in front of a group teaching obvious deceptive doctrines. Rather it will be someone who has already bought into a demonic lie and believed it to be the truth. Deception and error are smuggled in, intertwined with truth and are now taught to others as the real deal.

Notice verse 2 in 1 Timothy 4: "Speaking lies in hypocrisy; having their conscience seared with a hot iron;" One would think that people such as these would stand out like a sore thumb - horns on their head, hooves for feet and a spiked tail. But remember the warning back in 2 Peter 2:1 "false teachers among you."

> The responsibility for each of us is to hear the word, study the word, lay each teaching we receive alongside of the written word - the logos - and discern it for ourselves: does this teaching or prophetic word line up with scripture? Then, if we have any questions or doubts we are to bring it back to the teacher for clarity, not merely for argument sake. We will all have different points of view on scriptural meaning that do not warrant contention or major disputes (1 Cor. 1:11-18).

On the other hand there are times when we must choose to disagree and to let it be known to the teacher that we cannot embrace a certain doctrine or emphasis being promoted, at least for now in our understanding. How we disagree makes all the difference in the world. As believers, we are called to walk in peace with one another and any truth we speak must be with the grace of God and not a Pharisaical "better than thou" spirit (Ephesians 4:15).

We are all prone to making mistakes and, like it or not, our understanding of scripture is limited, and it is limited for two reasons that I can think of at this moment. One, is the obvious, our natural ability to read scripture and understand it with all its Hebrew and Greek renderings in the light of our present understanding and circumstances. The key word for all of us is "limited." Did not Jesus rebuke the finest scholars of His day? He taught them that in the case of the woman who married seven brothers in succession after the previous one had passed away. The Pharisees had come to their own conclusion based on their understanding of the scriptures. Those who questioned Him thinking they had the answer were most likely shocked when they were told "you are mistaken not understanding the Scriptures, or the power of God" (Matt. 22:29). This is just one example of many where someone was corrected for their limited understanding of scripture concerning God's power.

The second reason points to the revelation side of scripture. This is the God-breathed side of scripture. How many of us can account for the myriads of time the Holy Spirit 'quickened' our understanding of a certain verse or portion of Scripture that just seemed to say what it said with nothing more? Then after the Lord opened it up to us, it became alive and full of meaning beyond the obvious rendering on the page. In Luke 24:45 it reads, "Then He (Jesus) opened their minds to understand the Scriptures...."

The latter part of verse 32 reads "...while He was explaining (or literally opening) the Scriptures to us...." Again in John 14:26: "But the Helper, the Holy Spirit, whom the Father will send in My name, He will teach you all things and bring to your remembrance all that I have said to you." This would certainly include all the words that Jesus spoke in Scripture but with the added "opening" of their minds included.

There is another point that I think would help illuminate the work of the Holy Spirit. In John 16:13 the KJV reads, "howbeit when he, the Spirit of truth is come, he will guide you into all truth: for he shall not speak of himself; but whatsoever he shall hear, that shall he speak: and he will show you things to come." I believe this verse strengthens the idea that to truly understand God's word we must receive that enlightenment from the Holy Spirit. There are two words in this verse that I will use their Greek meanings to amplify this same thought.

> "He will guide you..." - that word guide in the Greek is *hodegeo* and it means to lead the way, to guide the blind, to lead or guide a traveler through an unknown country by means of the safest course. The other word is "show"- "...He will show you things to come." The word show is the Greek word *ang-el'-lo* which means to announce, declare, rehearse, report or speak.

Again our understanding of scripture is dependant on our willingness to let the Holy Spirit lead us as those who really can't see very well and are not sure where they are going. The Holy Spirit will also announce to us that which He hears from the Godhead and will reveal to us things that will happen in the future. This is the prophetic flow of the Spirit in the individual as well as the Church.

Where then is the balance between "contending for" and just agreeing to disagree?

Is there such a line in the sand? Are we not all students in the process of being taught and educated in, as my first Pastor would say, the "school of hard knocks" - our lives?

What I believed firmly yesterday I am not so sure of today; it seems life, circumstances and maturity have given me a different perspective on this verse or that scripture! Some things change while others things cannot, and by this I mean, in particular, some of the cornerstone truths of scripture that must not be allowed to be packed up and moved to the attic because they are inconvenient or they make people uncomfortable. It is at this juncture that we must hold the ground; this has to be our line in the sand; this error must stop here and advance no further.

The cross, as I have mentioned earlier, is the one area that I will focus on in this work. The church is in a fight for its very life and identity, a struggle it has endured and overcome throughout the centuries. Not against new enemies but against the same old ones, dressed up and packaged differently but still subtle, insidious and dangerous.

This struggle is not so much with an outside force clearly distinguished as foe but is with an 'inborn child' with a spiritual genetically-altered mission trying desperately to reprogram the original template and present a different Jesus and a very different Gospel back to the Church and to the world.

An Outdated Gospel

> It is a new 'user friendly' type of Christianity that does not rub anyone the wrong way; in fact, it would never try to make anyone feel bad about sin or their own wrongdoing. We are all one big happy family never wanting to point out the obvious elephants in the rooms of our lives. This seeker friendly evolving hybrid mixture in its truest sense seeks its own way - a new freedom not taught in scripture.

Paul in his letter to the Philippians church wrote, "But I hope in the Lord Jesus to send Timothy to you shortly, so that I may be encouraged when I learn of your condition. For I have no one else of kindred spirit who will genuinely be concerned for your welfare. For they all seek after their own interest, not those of Christ Jesus" (Phil. 2:19-21). Paul's great concern was that there were very few who were willing to represent the true interest of the Gospel in an accurate manner no matter what the cost would be and not their own self-serving interest.

The 'new gospel' is all about putting a positive spin on just about anything one could do, that as human beings there is nothing inherently wrong with us other than maybe we've just had a bad day and we are the victims of… you name it! We're just reacting to our hostile environment. No blame to take, no wrongdoing on our part for any of our actions, and certainly nothing to be ashamed of or to be sorry about.

The new packaged gospel leaves the person's sin intact. The new message does not make any demands and yet it is powerless to truly set anyone free. The Savior in this rendition looks and sounds more like a "flower child" of the sixties exclaiming the peace and love mantra than the rugged carpenter from Galilee commanding His followers to repent of their sins and to take up their cross and follow Him. However, this old and so-called outdated message is and will remain the one that delivers the goods.

This is not a matter of preference as if all the message options produce similar results. They do not and they cannot. That is the reason they come packaged in a similar paper to give the appearance of being the same. However similar they may appear to be, the substance inside is the difference between life and death.

Before we move on to take a closer look at the next chapter, I want to close with two scripture verses that so aptly apply to this day and age even as they did in St. Paul's day.

"For the word of the cross is to those who are perishing foolishness, but to those who are being saved it is the power of God." (1Cor. 1:18 NASB)

"...but we preach Christ crucified, to Jews a stumbling block and to Gentiles foolishness." (1 Cor. 1: 23 NASB)

The cross has always been an offensive and foolish message to the crowds and even to the disciple who tend to follow at a distance, yet it remains the "power of God" to those disciples who long after son-ship and intimacy with the Father. The road less travelled yields in time a bountiful treasure of righteousness as we press in to gaze at the matchless beauty of the Lord.

> Our responsibility as individual Christians can seem somewhat foreboding, even overwhelming. And one of the greatest tragedies today is that a whole generation of believers is left in their own compromised condition not having heard the whole truth. By not understanding the power of the Cross at work in their own lives, they will be left to battle a war without the divine weapons designed to 'take the field'.

Without a Cross message, how does one teach death to self, and if this is lacking or absent how is our old nature dealt with let alone the temptations of everyday? If the old nature is still alive and our flesh remains uncrucified, what is the condition of the church? There can be no going on to a mature man or woman in Christ.

The New Testament church in the Book of Acts must continue to be our model. Whatever is new or emerging in this modern church had better have the old rugged cross at the heart of its message. A new generation of believers is being duped into embracing a good 'ole boy' God who wants to make everybody feel at home in whatever sin they may be bound with and who places no demands on anyone to change or conform to His word. This is an old lie.

We do not have a grandfather type of God wringing His hands hoping His kids will not get upset with Him. He is not a benign, powerless character who only waves His wand to bless one and all even though they may engage in questionable lifestyles and practices contrary to His word. Our God is an awesome God, one to whom generations of believers have bowed low with reverent fear and honor, where saints of old fell down before Him as dead men and all their strength drained away.

Oh how the Church needs to pick up their Bibles again and begin to read of this Majestic God and return to a place of brokenness and humility. And maybe, just maybe, the Glory of the Lord will fill the House once again.

Chapter 3

Nevertheless Not My Will

The cross on which Jesus died was a well planned, well orchestrated event that was actually in the mind of God before the beginning of time. Often when we speak of a cross we may simply focus on the wooden crossbeams as a structure of wood made by the Romans to torture their victims by crucifixion. However, this conclusion would only be partially correct and, worst of all, would miss the much larger truth taught throughout scripture.

I would describe the true meaning of the cross as a collision of two wills followed by the emergence of only one. Understand, that in the process of one will emerging, there will be sorrow and suffering on our part as the Cross claims its victim, inevitably. Let us also understand that the principle of the Cross is firmly taught and embraced in scripture. However, the divine application of the cross and its many aspects stretches out over a vast array of life experiences and seasons.

When you ask two or more people to draw up a plan of some sort, whether business, construction, even a religious plan, we all know it will not take long before disagreement shows its pretty face. Realistically, before the work proceeds, the parties involved will need to make concessions. There will need to be a give and take attitude or this endeavor will "bite the dust".

This process of working together with a group does bear fruit. Drawing from a pool of wisdom and experience should be an asset and not a deficit. No one understands this better than those who have worked long hours and sacrificed a whole lot of time and energy to hammer out plans, contracts or policies of some sort. Everyone on such a committee knows all too well that this was a team effort; everyone who has a stake in this plan had a voice at the table; their views were heard even if not all of their input was implemented.

This is a pattern of democracy - the voice of the people and the power of the people.

It is the greatest and most powerful form of government on the planet. When everyday citizens of a nation know that they have a stake in the future of their nation or corporation and that their voice is a deciding factor in the direction that nation, business or union will take you can be sure that most individuals feel a personal responsibility to cast their vote or voice their opinion and beliefs. The benefits or consequences in time will reflect their choices, good or bad.

In the Kingdom of God, democracy does not exist: it is a non-entity. And Christians quite often remain incredulous about this absolute. The decisions, the laws and the plans of God for people, governments and nations will not be confirmed or rejected with our vote. What may be a great form of government on the earth is of little concern in God's eternal plan. Even before we had a chance to agree with it or give it our thumbs down, He set out His plan for us before the foundations of the world.

> The one voice that rings in the Father's heart and brings Him great delight is the voice of the child of God who has learned to echo the voice of the "firstborn Son". We read in Psalms 40:7, 8: "Then I (Jesus) said Behold I come; In the scroll of the book, it is written of me; I delight to do Thy will, O my God; Thy law is written in My heart."

Every time I read this verse, I think of Jesus in the circumstances and situations of His life and I hear this eternal truth proclaimed out of His mouth. This was His mandate from heaven. This was Mr. Phelps's "Mission Impossible" which always began with a short audio tape with instructions for his next mission, and included the disclaimer "if you should decide to do it..." leaving room for him to choose to take on the mission or reject it altogether. Similarly, the Father, before time began, had the mission for His Son, His beloved Son, all planned:

'Son, (can you hear the Father asking His Son) I want you to take this mission to go to the earth. It requires you to humble yourself and take the form of the man we've created. You will have to leave all of your divine powers behind with me. There is one more thing I must tell you; you will suffer greatly, in fact at one point, I am telling you now, you're going to ask me if this whole ordeal can be passed over and if there can be another way to redeem man, our creation. I know that we both are of one mind and heart in this matter and that's why it must be you'.

With a little imagination I hear Jesus exclaim with all the confidence the eternal Son of God can muster (and that is a whole lot), 'Father I have come to do your will and your will alone. This is what is beating in my heart; I have no other agenda than to give my life for our creation and to follow your every word and instruction to advance your kingdom and your will in the earth and in the hearts and minds of man.

Two thousand years ago, Jesus begins the mission and as we read in the recorded pages of scripture, we are often times reminded of a Son whose only purpose was to do the will of His Father and He did not depart from this path.

Here are a few key scriptures that Jesus spoke clearly stating and revealing the heart of the Son of Man: "Jesus therefore answered and was saying to them, Truly, truly I say to you, the Son can do nothing of Himself unless it is something He sees the Father doing for whatever the Father does, these things the Son also does in like manner" (John 5: 19). We could translate this verse to read, 'I don't do anything unless I see My Father do it first.'

Another example: Jesus said, "Therefore, when you lift up the Son of Man, than you will know that I am He, and I do nothing on My own initiative, but I speak these things as the Father taught Me" (John 8:28). Here again we could paraphrase like this: 'I don't start anything on My own, I only speak the things My Father has taught Me, you will realize this later after I'm crucified.'

His only agenda was to please the Father! This encompassed a great deal but it still boiled down to one thing; there was no straying off course, not even for a moment. There was no pursuing any personal desires or self-interest. His focus was as sharp as a laser beam as He says, "I did not speak on My own initiative, but the Father Himself who sent Me has given Me commandment, what to say, and what to speak" (John12:49). Once again Jesus reiterates only speaking and saying what the Father is telling Him, but in this verse Jesus tells us that this isn't just a great idea for Him to do, but this is by way of "commandment". The Strong's Concordance renders commandment as: an injunction, authoritative, a charge. Jesus said His Father commanded His words and actions; He did not initiate or begin anything of His own accord.

We look at these verses and we cringe inside; we all know that we have not come under such a 'holy restraint'; none of us has embraced obedience to this degree. In fact, deep down we believe we cannot achieve this. However, the hard truth may be that why we cannot is actually, because we will not. We tell ourselves there is no way we can adhere to His commands so why try.

One reason, and there are a few, why we believe we can't is because sometimes as we look to the will of the Father we see it more as heavy and burdensome, a task we have to perform and accomplish for God.

> In much of our thinking, we are still under a law mentality. There is not always a great deal of delight in doing the will of God; it comes down as more of a drudgery much like the 'children of Israel' who moaned and complained at every turn and bump. What was it about Jesus who could say "I delight to do Thy will..."? Is this kind of testimony reserved for Jesus alone? Is there a possibility that we, and please hear me, believe we cannot have this resolve, only because it is not our one genuine goal? The true indicator of being in that intimate relationship is when we are no longer able to resist the Father's gentle nudge on our hearts.

Jesus lived in this 'secret place' He didn't come to earth with an 'I have to' attitude, a duty mindset or a taking care of daddy's business orientation. No, Jesus took it from the place of a life lived in close proximity where His gaze never left the Courts of heaven and out of that place He could say 'I can only say those things I hear My Father saying to Me. It is the ongoing dialogues we are having together and I can only move in the direction of pleasing Him more than meeting My own life requirements' (my paraphrase).

Meek is a word which carries a volume of meaning beyond our English language translations. We have understood 'meek' to mean gentle, humble and even weak.

However, the Vines Expository of Biblical Words renders meek as follows;"meek (praotes gr.) the inwrought grace of the soul; and the exercises of it are chiefly towards God. It is the temper of the spirit in which we accept His dealings with us as good and therefore without disputing. This meekness however, being first of all meekness before God is also such in the face of men, even evil men, out of a sense that these with the insults and injuries which they inflict are permitted and employed by Him(God) for the chastening and purifying of His elect"

This characteristic describes Jesus to the letter in His responses to His Father and His will. Jesus was not weak in the Garden of

Gethsemane He could have called twelve legions of angels to protect and deliver Him. All power and authority was at His disposal yet at no point did He assert Himself and move out on His own revealing self interest or preservation. He was at rest and deemed His Fathers purposes and dealings as good and without disputing them.

There is a 'Oneness' that is only understood when a certain will is eliminated - ours. Until then, there is an internal disconnect resulting in a task mentality which originates from the natural man – the 'self man'- and unless that man is broken and His will is relinquished to the Father that union will evade him. We cannot bypass the crosses of our lives; they are custom made vehicles that will usher us into the presence of God and also allow us to remain there. We should not be surprised that after consecrating our lives these custom made vehicles suddenly pull up next to us, like someone calling for a taxi, ready to take us where Christ has already gone, to the wilderness!

The new emphasis on seeker friendly churches will one day pay the costliest price. By side stepping the cross and allowing the natural man to live, they choose a 'cross-less' gospel, forfeiting the only access into an ongoing rich communion with the Father in order to please the passing whims of their carnal, self serving man.

The process of 'son ship' is second to none. Without the same intent as Jesus, we will be diverted by a hundred and one distractions and pulled in every direction, all away from communion with the Father.

I am not talking about performance at this juncture. What I am talking about is intent, a heart that is set, the eye of the heart being fixed on Jesus Christ. We have to begin with an honest desire to obey with an intent to embrace all that the Father has determined for us and the transforming power He will use to bring it all about (Colossians 3:1-3).

We are always so focused on accomplishing, doing something for God. God on the other hand like any master craftsman is not in a hurry to get it done. His name is on the bottom line; His work will be accomplished with excellence. We must learn to trust God in the process. In time, He will make room for us to bear fruit that will remain.

This process is the metamorphoses of Romans 12:2. We are exhorted "not to be conformed to this world", not to be fashioned after the same pattern as the world, "but, [to] be transformed by the renewing of [our] mind...", to be transfigured and changed, to go from a caterpillar stage to a butterfly stage. Remember our early science classes. The end goal for us is the same image as Jesus Christ - from where we are now to where He is - by the renewing or renovating of our minds.

Salvation is the first necessary step on the road to transformation of mind and heart. Most of us get this far. Our peril at this point is to think that we have arrived into the Kingdom as sons and daughters. However, we have only stepped into the doorway. Salvation is the initial work of the cross; Christ died on the cross in our place to remove the judgment from over us, the Father placed it on Jesus alone. This saving grace was then realized in our lives the moment we accepted Jesus into our hearts and repented of our sins.

The Cross of Christ provides more than just salvation and the forgiveness of sin. In that glorious work, we have also been given all manner of grace and power to live godly, disciplined and overcoming lives for the Lord. The Cross, which has manifold aspects of power and authority, releases abilities (or another word that would more accurately describe this is spiritual muscle power) to live above the defeated mindset of so many (Titus 2:12-14).

The same Spirit that led Jesus into the wilderness for forty days in order to try Him wants to lead us into the wildernesses of His design that He might reveal to us the things that are in our hearts. Coming into the Kingdom is great but we can still remain as spiritual brats for decades, always demanding that God do things our way, stomping our feet on the ground without concern for what God may be asking of us at any particular moment. The danger here is that we can press our own will on God and desire to push the envelope to the edge oblivious to the fact, He is actually leading us is in the way of life. Many times, what we may be insisting on may turn out to cost us more than we bargained for.

Jesus said in the garden, "nevertheless not My will be done but yours...." What we express in our 'gardens of testing' reveal whose will is really of the upmost importance to us. The children of Israel, as they wandered around the desert, never set the intent of their heart on God. In fact, God reveals the true intent of their heart in this verse: "their heart was far from me." It was nothing more than lip service. A whole lot of people (God's people) wandering around the desert after witnessing the most astounding miracles and still their hearts could not embrace the laws and precepts of this mighty God except for Joshua, Caleb and Moses. It says of Joshua and Caleb that they were of a different spirit (Numbers14:24).

> A little observation I will tuck in here is that signs, miracles and wonders will not and cannot change our hearts, take a close look at the 'children of Israel.'

Again, this is not about doing everything right. Moses certainly did not and if we were to look at the great men and woman of faith we would soon see that their feet also were made of clay.

Before I get too far I just wanted to clarify that at the root of our unwillingness to abandon ourselves to the will of the Father is a deep-seated fear. Moreover, it is a fear that we are all too often unwilling to face. Christians, after all are not supposed to have fear, right? So what is this fear?

We used to sing this song many years ago and I had the hardest time singing this one part, and it was because I was afraid God would take me at my words and unleash a chain of events similar to Job pulverizing me as I sang. Here is a sample of that song. Maybe you sang it as well, or maybe you could not!

"and whatever it takes for my will to break, that's what I'll be willing to do. I'll trade sunshine for rain, life comforts for pain that's what I'll be willing to do...."

Apart from having a nice tune, I can only assume that at this refrain in the song everyone in the building was probably cringing with their fingers crossed in hopes that God would see the fingers and allow the angel of death to pass over.

But hold it! Fear of a good Father and His will for us? How can that be? Could it be that we have not come to know Him as we ought - as Jesus did?

Could this be the motivating factor behind some of these faith teachings: teachings that really do not leave any room for God to answer in some other way but ours? The authoritative tones we use to literally command God demonstrates that God is more like a heavenly genie or a butler only here to act on behalf of the owner.

There is a faith teaching that is truly Biblical and sound, and yes, even here, if we are not directed by the Holy Spirit in our faith whether it's laying hands on the sick or in prophetic words and utterances our faith may be just that - ours and ours alone. It is devoid of inspiration and will lack the divine impartation of His power to accomplish the very thing we may feel is God-breathed, all the while being a good idea and not a God idea and without any results. Let us be vigilant to follow the Holy Spirit and no other.

True faith is at rest in the will and purposes of God; true faith rests on the bosom of Jesus; fear has no place. Faith looks into the eyes of the Father and echo's the words of the first born son of God: "I pray that You would remove this cup from Me, nevertheless not My will but Yours be done." There is no striving to be out of what is Father's will; there is no arm-twisting. The relationship gives birth to an open heaven; "ask that your joy maybe made full." We have a generous Father who desires to give, so our asking must transcend our repetitious 'bless me, bless me' mindset.

When the two wills become one, the one will flows through the mind and heart of the believer with a real faith and confidence that he or she has heard what the Father is saying. From this place, we are able to watch what the Father is doing.

There is great error with the idea that because it is written in the Bible and God spoke it as a promise that it is automatically mine the moment I pray it or in some cases demand it to be done. On the other hand, it is required of us to seek God for all we're worth, to press into that holy place and receive a *'rhema'* word charged full of God's faith, not ours, a cupful of living promise and impartation out of the vast ocean of the *logos* of God's word, the Bible. Only this word of faith will move the mountains and all other impossible hurdles obstructing our ways.

One great concern that I would raise at this point: do we carry an inherent fear that keeps us from coming to that resting place in God and inhibits our ability to trust His will for us? I question if our many declarations of faith tend towards trying to create a God that takes on the form of our own image. I am not so sure we are at peace with a God who acts independently and is not accountable to us somehow.

The reason I venture to say this is that the great majority of us cannot bear the thought that God would allow us to suffer and to go through difficult things. Actually, we might even be horrified to find out that He is actually planning what some of us would consider very negative experiences. The Bible is literally full of examples of adverse things in the lives of "born again" believers – imagine that! We will take a closer look at these individuals a little later, but right now, I would add that our prayers are many times tainted with self-preservation and a whole lot of self-serving.

Could it be possible we are trying to direct God somewhat on what we want as opposed to what He wants? Do we take our cues from Him or does He take them from us? So begins our repetitious requests trying to change God's mind in a particular area, a bombardment meant to avert internal visions we've created in our minds that God is out to squash us or make our lives miserable and if we just hammer at this long enough, perhaps He will change His mind. This is a recipe for frustration.

With that 'God breathed' word of God, we will have the inner knowing, witness and leading of the Holy Spirit as we move forward to fight ensnarements, obstacles and demonic strategies designed to harm and destroy us. Indeed this is not possible without the guidance of the Holy Spirit. This is about moving in the wisdom and discernment of God, we need to be able to distinguish the genuine leading of His Spirit from that which has its roots in our own flesh or is instigated by the demonic realms or both.

> We have been conditioned here in North America with a feel good Gospel so that when something unsettling and disturbing comes our way we find ourselves automatically rebuking the devil and his cohorts. However, let us get back to the Son of God and look at some scriptures concerning what Jesus suffered through for our salvation as our example.

"Fixing our eyes on Jesus, the author and perfecter of faith, who for the joy set before Him endured the cross despising the shame, and has sat down at the right hand of the throne of God" (Hebrews 12:2). Jesus did not enjoy the cross, He endured it. Yet He remained under it and bore it. The joy, the delight was set before Him and after His death He took His place at the right hand of the throne of God.

Hebrews 12:3 "For consider Him who has endured such hostility by sinners against Himself, so that you may not grow weary and lose heart." We are asked to take time to consider the suffering Jesus went through at the hands of sinners; we are not talking crucifixion yet, but the strife, contradiction, the betrayal the lies and the abuse - physical, mental, emotional and spiritual, just to name a few. Why are we asked to do so? The latter part of the verse explains: so that we may not grow weary and lose heart. We are told to look at Jesus as our example on how to go through our crosses and sufferings and to not become worn out and be dismayed.

In verse four, we're told that in our striving against sin we have not resisted or withstood to the point of shedding our own blood. In our battles to live holy and righteous lives we have not been so pressed on every dimension both natural and spiritual where our bodies, under such stress, perspired blood.

In the next few verses, the author of Hebrews is trying to shed an important light on this whole subject of suffering and obedience. It is addressed to sons. Verses 5-6: "and you have forgotten the exhortation which is addressed to you as sons, 'My son, do not regard lightly the discipline of the Lord, nor faint when you are reproved by

Him; For those whom the Lord loves He disciplines and he scourges every son whom He receives.'"

Plainly stated, we have forgotten or we are, as the Greek renders forgotten, 'utterly oblivious' to the fact that the Lord chastens. The Greek rendering of chastening is "tutorage, education or training". (Vines)

We are not to regard it lightly when He convicts us or finds fault. He loves us and because He loves us (*agape*), He will scourge us in order to bring us near to Himself. Our willingness to embrace His discipline opens the way and creates a place where He will delight in us.

This is heavy stuff, but there is one thing we need to remember here. What God does with His sons is never about punishment. He may deal with rebels one way, but Sons are set aside under His divine tutorage and personal correction. The Greek rendering here is clear with the words used here: chastening, child training or, in other versions, discipline.

Again, we are prone to think in terms of God giving us a swat because we are out of line. The words scourge or flog usually conjure up all kinds of abusive images. This is not the intent. We need to take hold of the true picture of our heavenly Father. We see that even with the word "scourge", the Father's only purpose is to break us of our independent "lone ranger" mindset and bring us closer to Him. At times we will require some stiff correction to get our attention and to apprehend our hearts.

The complete picture is made a little clearer in verses 7, 8, 9 (You may want to study this chapter). Instead of a line-by-line analysis of the next few verses, I will summarize the thought behind the verses.

We endure this training, only because we are sons. Every father trains up his sons; that is obvious, and if we are unwilling to receive this training then can we really call ourselves sons? On the contrary, we would be illegitimate. So then, if our earthly fathers trained and educated us and we respected them for it, should we not submit even more to our Heavenly Father and His training and find life?

Remember what it said about Jesus "who for the joy set before Him endured the cross."

We read in verse 11 that all this discipline and training is not always joyful but sorrowful, but everyone who allows the Father to do what He wants to do will afterwards produce the peaceful fruit of righteousness.

> Jesus allowed the Father to place the cross on Him, and the untold sufferings that went along with it, so that ultimately this Son would take His place next to the Father on His throne. It is not all about signs, miracles and wonders as important as they may be. Our conformity to the image of the Son should be our number one mandate. I will venture to say that allowing ourselves to be conformed to the image of the Son and submitting to the Father's chastening will reveal the heart of a true Son.

Verse 6: "and He scourges every son He receives." This word 'receives' is rendered in Greek to mean "accept near, delight in." Being brought near and being delighted in by the Father is in my opinion the best place to be as a co-worker with the Holy Spirit. To be empowered to move into miracles, signs and wonders if He so chooses only because I have been brought near. And from this intimate relationship I will learn to know what my Heavenly Father is saying and doing about all the needs that surround me.

1 John 5:3 "For the true love of God is this; that we do His commands (keep His ordinances and are mindful of His precepts and teaching). And these orders of His are not irksome (burdensome, oppressive, or grievous). The Amplified Bible

Chapter 4

What About Me

Has there ever been more of an emphasis on 'self' than in our present generation? Inventions and every form of technology are exploding around us and I'm sure that we have seen only a glimpse of what is coming. But all of these things are manufactured and marketed with the purpose of making our lives simpler and easier in order to free us up to do the things we have always wanted to do: 'the sky is the limit'. It certainly is an age to marvel at; what the human mind can dream of, it will ultimately achieve and create.

Please do not misunderstand me; so much of what has been invented has made our lives here in the industrial nations and around the world a whole lot easier and certainly more comfortable, for which we as consumers are very thankful.

For better or for worse here in North America we have been liberated in relation to the amount of time and money we have to fritter doing the things we like. No other generation has been able to enjoy the luxury of working a set number of hours to then be able from those wages earned, turn around and splurge it on non essentials for the whole family like vacations, bigger and better toys, the multiple sports clubs for the kids, parties, trips and the list goes on and on. No doubt, we are a blessed and prosperous nation. One look around the world should crystallize an appreciation for what God has blessed us with here in North America.

"Blessed is the nation whose God is the Lord" (Ps.33:12). We are the recipients of God's love, favor and certainly His blessings. But I hope the outpouring of divine blessing upon this nation has not been, in our minds as Christians, due to our entitlement - a 'we deserve what we have' mentality.

> Our present day blessings in this land result, I believe, from our basic belief in and adherence to the laws and precepts of God as a society. What we are and what we have is based entirely on the multiple generations before us who sacrificed so much to establish and secure our religious heritage by honoring and exalting the Lord Jesus Christ.

Simultaneously the battle for the soul of our nation continues to rage. We are faced with a plurality of beliefs that overshadow the Christian faith assaulting and deriding its core values as outdated and even dangerous, if you can believe that. And much of this thinking comes from within the churches very own ranks!

Christians have always been in the minority; however the true saints of God throughout the centuries have not been dismayed by their numbers. Though many have claimed to believe, far less were willing to follow in the footsteps of the Master. This has always been the case.

In this twenty first century, we Christians in the western church will leave a legacy not only to our own children but also to the world at large, a testimony that will hopefully reflect a people of faith that have embraced the correct principles and truth of their God.

In Psalms 11:3 we read, "If the foundations are destroyed, what will the righteous do?" In reference to the church, I have tried in these opening chapters to underscore the assaults that are now trying to subvert the very bedrock of the Christian church since day one - the Cross. To remove this foundation would be similar to cutting loose the moorings of a great ship and watch it drift out into the open sea.

There are no substitutes for the work of the Cross in the believer's life. History will tell whether we are a Christ centered, God fearing people who preached the power of the Cross and stemmed the tide or whether we caved in to the narcissistic, self indulging spirit of this world that eventually permeated the body of Christ in the West unabated.

Our own ability to discern the times we live in and the true condition has been jaded somewhat. Can we really compare ourselves with ourselves; if we are both blind will we not both fall into the ditch? The issue is not so much that we do not know the standard or the right course to take, it is more a question of are we willing to deny ourselves by choosing the right course of action.

Take the medicine, yes it taste terrible but it will heal our infirmity. The medicine in this case is what the Lord prescribes to heal our many worldly and carnal 'afflictions' - His word. "From Your precepts I get understanding; Therefore I hate every false way."(Ps.119:104 NASB) There are no substitutes and yes, there are some side effects but in this case the side effects are not more serious than the illness. Yes, we may have dizzy spells and go through withdrawals because we're not getting our customary fix. But if we persist it won't be long after we've renounced some stuff – stuff we thought would give us life, joy and peace and thought it was O.K. with God - we will begin to experience a dimension of His presence we didn't think was possible.

Our pursuit of God is not rocket science; God has laid out some easy to follow instructions that are hinged to a close relationship with Him. The point being is that they are His instructions and not ours; they are not negotiable nor are they suggestions. If we set our minds to follow them, they always lead us to Him if we come at this with a right attitude of heart. This is the underlying problem in pursuing the Lord. We need to follow the instructions, follow the instructions, and follow the instructions.

> Our usual response to that idea is 'Lord what about me? I want to have a say in this process. This is my life, you know!' We just cannot seem to help it: we want to be a consultant to help the Holy Spirit and help Him direct our lives. We are not always vocal about our objections and our silent interjections but we hope that God gets our drift.

This one issue, the 'what about me issue', will be the one article that will continue to impede our progress in the Lord and many times bring it to a halt. 'What about me' is as real and as close as it gets to the tissue, blood, feelings and emotions all wrapped up in a sphere called our human body. Aspirations, dreams discouragement and failure proceed from the center of who we are, how we are and what we would like to be. Our pain is real, our happiness is real and our questions of why are also very real. At times, we know at least in part what He is asking but deep inside we wrestle with the finer points of our limited understanding on fairness and balance and when is enough - enough! We want to do His will but we are genuinely conflicted about how these trials or adversities will overwhelm us or push beyond our ability to cope.

Our natural knee jerk reaction will come from our 'view' of things. We object, we bargain we argue and at times, we break off the talks. In His loving kindness and patience, He waits for us and draws us to Himself in ways that bypass our abilities to comprehend them but He never lets go.

God does not dismiss the deep need for recognition, purpose, creativity and relevance. God does not see these as 'non issues'; His desires for us is not that we all unite into some mindless blob that relegates uniqueness and individualism as some devilish idea that must be crucified and die. He made us all unique and different. But at times I have struggled, wrestled and argued with God certain that He was out to destroy who I really was and make me just another cookie cut Christian devoid of character or personality. I wonder where that thought came from.

> My fight, although futile, was a process of recognizing that God was out to refine me, not destroy me and all that He created and destined for me to be and do was a larger event on His calendar than mine.

There is a place for the 'what about me' cry, a desire to do all and be all we have been gifted to be, but I believe in time it will give way to a higher reliance and a greater confidence in God as Jesus so correctly put it, "Nevertheless not My will be done but Yours." We have yet to be convinced of God's eternal goodness towards.

This is not to deny our humanity and the legitimate needs that we have as human beings. Jesus acknowledged this in several places in one instance; He said "Or what man is there among you, when his son shall ask him for a loaf, will give him a stone? Or if he ask for a fish, he will not give him a snake will he? If you then being evil, know how to give good gifts to your children, how much more shall your Father who is in heaven give what is good to those who ask Him" (Mathew 7:9-11)!

The point being God is not insensible to our needs. We have a 'good' God, as Paul wrote to the Philippians church that "shall supply all your needs according to His riches in glory in Christ Jesus" (Phil.4:19). He is a good Father who knows how to meet every requirement we will ever have, even to the point where He gives us the desires of our hearts. I sincerely believe that when we embrace His desires as our requirements then we shall have the desires of our hearts because we have the same heart and the same desires as the Father.

Jesus made it abundantly clear by further reiterating that birds don't store up food in barns or sow nor do they reap yet our heavenly Father feeds them, are we not worth more than they (Matt. 6:26)? So when do we become secure enough in the Father's goodness that we may all as weaned babies rest in His arms content and at rest?

Do we ever get beyond the daily 'I need' or 'what about me?' Does this cycle remain our prime focus throughout our lives? Our ongoing spiritual S.O.S. signal being sent out over the airwaves indicating to God what He already said He would supply and yet we continue to expend so much time and energy interceding for our needs.

This is the very point Jesus makes repeatedly in the Gospels about providing for us: "Do not be anxious then, saying, what shall we eat? Or what shall we drink? Or with what shall we clothes ourselves? For all these things the Gentiles eagerly seek; for your heavenly Father knows you need ALL these things. BUT SEEK

FIRST THE KINGDOM and HIS RIGHTEOUSNESS and ALL THESE THINGS SHALL BE ADDED UNTO YOU" (emphasis mine) (Matt 6:33). We can rest in the unchangeable truth of His word and character, since He already knows our needs He has already arranged to provide them.

The prominent theme in much of our preaching and teaching across our fruited plain has often times kept us focused on the earthly. We have become so blessing oriented that our pursuit has shifted from the Lord to the fringe benefits of serving Him. Of course, as I have stated there is nothing wrong with benefits and blessings: they are the gifts of a wonderful Dad. However, our concern should be this: are these good things igniting in me a deeper love and passion for Jesus or have I become somewhat distracted by them and they are now my primary pursuit?

> Many Christians in the west have accepted the notion that because God has been faithful by providing us all manner of good things that somehow this is some kind of barometer that He is pleased with where we are with Him in terms of our relationship as individuals and corporately as a church. God provides for us because He is good and faithful not because we are. He remains true to His good character.

We have measured our spirituality by the amount of toys and material goods we have attained or should I say, received, and this type of spiritual compass will give us a false reading every time. It seems we have become stuck in the mud here and we cannot seem to get our feet on a higher standpoint to see how magnificent this infinite God really is outside of just providing fish and loaves.

"Your fathers ate the manna in the wilderness and they died, I am the living bread that came down out of heaven; if any one eats of this bread, he shall live forever; and the bread also that I shall give for the life of the world is My flesh" (John 6:49-51). We may be fed and well taken care of, nevertheless we will perish if we never truly 'ate' of His flesh and 'drank' His blood. Jesus rebuked His followers for seeking Him only because He had fed them (John 6:26).

He was trying to awaken in them a desire for more than just satisfying their natural appetites. Our hunger will never be satisfied and our thirst never quenched at this level of seeking Him if it is only for the things He provides.

"Eating His flesh" and "drinking His blood" is a dimension of relationship that sounds intriguing and yet somewhat mystical (or perhaps horrifying to some). But it is very much like "seek first the kingdom of God and all these things shall be added unto you." God is inviting us to more of who He is beyond just provision. The children of Israel never came into that place, although it was available to them. This is the place of fellowship, the place of rest from our own striving.

"Since therefore it remains for some to enter it, and those who formerly had good news preached to them failed to enter because of disobedience" (Hebr. 6:16). It remains for us today to enter a rest from our own ways, our ends, and agendas and of our own self- made programs that exalt the flesh. The children of Israel are our example in many ways; they heard the 'good news' but failed to come into God's provision for them. We must come in order to cease from our constant human activity and human energy. "For the one who has entered His rest has himself also rested from his works, as God did from His. Let us therefore be diligent to enter that rest, lest anyone fail through following the same example of disobedience" (Hebr.5:10-11).

The Bible in an interesting way serves as a record of our Family Tree; it records a pattern that repeats itself from cover to cover about our human nature and its many shortcomings. We are confronted with the problems but thank God, we also have the remedy.

There is a country and western song years ago that said, "I beg your pardon, I didn't promise you a rose garden, along with the sunshine there has to be a little rain sometimes." The sun does not always shine nor does it always rain. This is also true in the Kingdom. As wonderful as those sunny days may be, it usually takes the stormy days to awaken in us an appetite and longing for more of

God. God did not promise us smooth sailing, but He did promise to get us over to the other side in the same boat as Him.

> Since we really do not understand all of God's ways and don't really know how He's bringing us into conformity with Him by methods He will use, we need to sit back and leave the driving to God. Once we come to this juncture of letting God take the helm - and it may require a few trips to the wilderness to release our tight grip - we will behold a dimension of God's 'rest' in our hearts beyond anything we have known.

This is a sample prayer for anyone who has come to a place where they are tired of the 'give me, give me' cycle and would like to come in to a more passionate place with God:

'What about me Lord? I realize that You will take care of all my needs. Thank you; I really appreciate your faithfulness and love. But what about this deep longing inside of me that nothing seems to satisfy? I know there has to be more; I feel unsettled within my spirit and yet there is this knowing that You are the only One that can satisfy my soul. I am not at peace inside only because this stirring urges me on to what I am not sure but I truly sense this is You tugging at me. I want to do something big for You or become someone great, yet I know somehow that's not what Your after. So I ask You Lord to draw me to Yourself in ways that I may never have imagined. I don't want to fear Your way or plan; I'm aware now that there will be a price and I'm O.K. with that. I only know I must have more of You.'

> There is no way a person can explain this deep sense of being drawn to more of God other than to echo what the Bible describes as "deep calling out to deep". There is a dimension to Christianity that has been labeled as radical, deep, mystical – meant, I suppose, to be in some way derogatory. I would venture to say that these radical, deep mystics just happen to be more desperate for God than the rest of the bunch.

Let me say this here lest I be misunderstood: these so called 'super' spiritual beings are not the product of their own inner strength or of their own fortitude as noble as that might sound. We are all entirely of the same human caliber. Unless the Spirit of God in us draws us to deeper and higher places in Him, we would have all parked the bus a longtime ago and camped out in 'Passive Park'(Rom.8:15). There can be no exaltation of man anywhere along the road to the mountain of God.

What was awakened in us at the 'new birth' the Holy Spirit has been faithful to fan even though the embers many times came close to dying out. But some choose not to be deterred no matter what comes along to distract them.

"For I am confident of this very thing, that He who began a good work in you will perfect it until the day of Jesus Christ" (Phil.1:6). This will always be a God work, just like the children of Israel. They were led out to the desert by God, fed by God, sustained with good health and in every other way blessed by God. They had no clue where they were going and how to get there, let alone stay alive on the journey: it was all God. This is exactly our case; our spiritual life and health can only be sustained and maintained by God Himself. We haven't the slightest clue what God will implement to set our course in His direction and what circumstances He will use to fashion us after Himself. Is it any wonder we call it 'a walk of faith'?

The humdrum and routine of everyday life has a way of lulling us to sleep. We tend to forget the impossibilities that God walks us through on a regular basis. Detestable as they maybe, it is the crisis moments in our lives that bring us back into a realistic perspective as to how big God really is.

Each one of us should go around to unsaved friends and family and people at work and take a poll on a few different topics about life in general just to see if there really is a difference between saved and unsaved. Now I'm sure we are, for the most part, well aware of the mental, physical and emotional health of others if we just tune in now and again to their conversations.

Here is a sample of what we might hear:
- "My kids are driving me crazy, they are so demanding so disrespectful."
- "My husband is always gone out with the boys; he never seems to take time with me anymore."
- "My wife, she doesn't understand me, she just nags all the time."
- "It seems we argue about everything, we can't agree on anything."
- "I'm sick for worrying about my daughter she out half the night."

We look at these samples and say wait a minute those issues are what we are experiencing now, never mind people in the world. So what is the difference then? The major difference is that we have a Father in heaven that is working all things together for good to those who love Him and are called according to His purposes. The world has no such recourse (Romans 8:28).

Christians have problems that are similar to those who make no profession of faith, why is that? First, we are all human; we all live on the same planet; we were all born in sin - none are good not one. Then miraculously we received Christ as our Savior and slowly but surely He began to put things back in order. Not all our baggage showed up in one night and so it will take a while for God to restore life and order in place of chaos and death. Christians are all still very human with a whole lot of dysfunctional issues that resemble others in the world - the very place God saved us from not so long ago.

So what is the difference? Again, we have a whole lot of similarities and that is my point; we sometimes believe that we become 'divine beings' the moment we accept Christ as our Savior and all our problems are just supposed to be cast into the sea at our command. When this fails to happen, we double our efforts and keep trying, hoping things will change. In time we begin to realize that problems just do not disappear, they are for the most part worked through by the grace and mercy of God for the transformation of our character and by a mind renewed by His Word in the constraints of each problem.

> No we are not 'divine beings' that are all powerful able to change events and circumstances by speaking scriptures into them trying to obliterate them like a spiritual bazooka just because we don't like what's going on around us. On the other hand, we are 'partakers' of the divine nature. The Greek word for partaker is '*koinonos*' which describes a sharer, a companion, a partner. We have been brought into fellowship with Christ to share the privileges and favor of His divine, nature not our own contrary to popular teaching.

Yes there are times, at the direction of the Holy Spirit, that we pray, intercede and speak to demonic entities to 'pull down' their destructive strategies and plans against us or others. We are not free to just rail and pray against inconvenient situations because they frustrate and test us. The prayers led by the Holy Spirit will be divinely powerful to secure the answer we are praying into, to see the miraculous changes and to alter the spiritual landscape over our lives and others.

The only thing divine about us is the Holy Spirit that dwells within. God's Spirit in us is all powerful, almighty, all knowing and all everything else that is in accordance to His nature. However His Spirit in us is still His Spirit in us, not our spirit hovering about leading us into our own campaigns and agendas and hoping that the Holy Spirit will approve of our presumptuous plans.

To receive the blessing and favor of the Lord we will have to allow His Spirit to lead. We who are in the growth development stages of walking with Him are being educated about who we are in Christ. In our training, we come to realize in time, hopefully, how small we really are. This is by no means a put down, but a revelation we need to embrace. Actually this is a safety zone: to know where our limits stop and where His begin. Do Not Touch His Glory. The bottom line remains the same; it is and will always be all about Him.

We will walk in all He has called us to walk in; He enlarges us in spirit, truth, understanding, He heals us, delivers us, blesses us in innumerable ways, leads us into path of righteousness and so much more. God is taking care of our 'what about me syndrome.'

Someone once said 'the bigger I grow in God the smaller I become"; this will be the testimony of all the saints of every age as we stand in awe one day no longer seeing Him through a glass darkly, One whose beauty, splendor and majesty are unequalled, unapproachable and overwhelming. This should also be I believe the testimony of the church now.

For too long the church has bought into a false notion of trying to impress God with what we can do for Him; He is impressed with us not for our doing but our being. We are His, loved and cared for; we have nothing to offer Him but ourselves.

> For too long we have tried to get His attention by trying to have faith and trying to believe for the impossible. All along, He has wanted us to acknowledge our inability to 'believe enough', to stop trying to draw from our own well that could not produce the life and power we needed for the moment, to humble ourselves in our crucible of life and take hold of Him in the crisis of our need and refuse to be dissuaded until His answer wrapped in His word is received. His attention has been on us even though our many appeals at times may have seemed to go unanswered.

An Outdated Gospel

For too long we have preached this gospel that exalts the creatures rather than the Creator, elevating them to some divine status and expending so much time and energy trying to become something they were never meant to be, bypassing His appeals to simply and humbly come to Him, and thus missing the rest and intimacy of His abiding place. We are fashioned to follow Him, not to lead Him.

For too long our emphasis has been self-focused and our gaze turned inward - the result of having gleaned over hundreds of success oriented materials intent on building the man and woman of God to be 'somebody'. Yet on this same road we call life, the Christ came and made Himself of no reputation to the point of becoming a lowly servant. How vastly different from our own emphasis. In fact, there is little resemblance in a large majority of the Western church to what we would read in our Bibles concerning denying ourselves taking up our crosses and following Jesus to what is actually taught.

Remember it was the Pharisees that caused Jesus so much grief and worked their strategy to have Him killed. Those same Pharisees walked around with a little box secured to their arms and their foreheads. All symbolic of their obedience to God with the idea that God's word was entering their minds and thus renewing their thoughts - a kind of osmosis I guess. On their arms it was symbolic that they were there to serve and use their lives in helping people; they were a special class, girded on the outside with the word of God. But this was nothing but an outward religious symbol that had no transforming effect on the inside.

On the flip side of this picture in today's church world we find a similar occurrence. Could we be guilty of something similar to the Pharisees when we quote and declare scripture all the while walking about with a resistant attitude to the will of God? Do we sense His leading but are actively trying to alter the outcome by declaring His word towards Him in an attempt to modify His will? Do we sidestep areas of His conviction or refuse to obey Him in areas that may require we set our lives in holy order in some way or other? Scary indeed!

Taking every thought captive to the obedience of Christ I believe means just that - every thought! We do not always know what spirit we are of or what inner influences motivate us. Remember this story: "Lord, do you want us to command fire to come down from heaven and consume them. But He turned and rebuked them." We do not always know what spirit is influencing us (Luke 9:54-55).

> Our human nature will always be with us; we cannot be not delivered of it though we might wish it at times. Though we are born again, our flesh will literally try to run the show to the point of squeezing Christ right out of our lives. We should not be surprised at this statement. One honest look at our inner appetites will reveal a major conflict of interest of spirit and flesh.

Paul in Galatians 5 exhorts us to "walk by the Spirit and you will not carry out the desire of the flesh." The word desire in the New American Standard Bible would read 'lust' in the King James, which tends to bring a darker side to this verse. The word lust in Greek is *'epithumia'* and is made up of two words:
- *epi*: which means, over
- *thumos*: which means, a craving, urge, a passion or a longing.

These two words together bring out the idea of being 'overly excited' over or for something, in this case our carnal desires. When we put these two words together in this verse it gives us a clearer or sharper meaning that would sound something like this: 'walk in the Spirit and you will not fulfill, accomplish or perform the fervent, passionate obsessive desire of your flesh.' The bottom line being our flesh has a mind of its own and it will take us where we may have wanted to go at one time, but now we are desire to bring our whole being under the control of the Holy Spirit and walk in paths of righteousness for His name sake.

Walking in the Spirit is about our lives being lived in close proximity to God and the things of God. We are new creations with new desires that are no longer under the control of the devil. We are no longer free to do our own thing or to serve our carnal nature even though it will fight us at every turn to get us to indulge in past practices that opened the door to sin or were just outright sin. Our new nature will desire the things of God, so we must be vigilant to walk down the center of the road trying to avoid all the ditches.

Walking in the Spirit is about coming under the disciplined walk of God's Holy Spirit; it is about obedience and submission to the voice of the Holy Spirit and about remaining 'hidden' in that grace provided to stay in victory and walk in holiness.

"But [like a boxer]I buffet my body [handle it roughly, discipline it by hardships] and subdue it, for fear that after proclaiming to others the Gospel and things pertaining to it, I myself should become unfit [not stand the test, be unapproved and rejected as a counterfeit]" (1 Cor.9:27 The Amplified Bible).

We are co laborers with Christ in the transformation of our minds; we must renew our minds (Romans12:2).

We must take every thought captive to the obedience of Christ (2 Cor.10:5).

We must renounce the hidden works of darkness in our lives presently and any who would seek to infiltrate us in the future (Romans 13:12).

This is all done in conjunction with the Holy Spirit leading, illuminating and empowering. We are not a self made spiritual man or woman, but we are being made into spiritual men and woman by the Spirit of God.

"Take My yolk upon you, and learn from Me, for I am gentle (meek) and humble in heart; you shall find rest for your souls" (Matt. 11:29).

Think of Jesus who resigned His life and will to the Father, standing silent before Pilate. Could He not have made a defense for Himself and convinced the mob by word or miracle that He was not a false teacher or false prophet? He could have performed a miracle for Herod who was so desirous to see Him and maybe set Him free for impressing royalty. But no, Jesus was at rest in the purposes of

God no matter what they appeared to be or how 'out of hand' things seem to get for Him.

> Our fears stem from this very fact that somehow we could find ourselves in circumstances that may have caught God off guard leaving us in a situation completely at the mercy of man or in some demonic trap suddenly sprung on us. To believe this notion would be to dismiss scripture and God's all inclusive abilities to protect, care and deliver us from any peril.

We must make room for the theology that God will not only allow but will also lead us into situations that may diminish our natural man but will cause our 'inner' man to rise up in strength and might. This is not about leading us into temptation; some might contest that anything negative or naturally harmful to me as a person somehow cannot be God.

> In God's eternal purposes for us He has often time had to turn a deaf ear to our many objections about our present circumstances so that a more superlative way would be revealed to us. Our momentary discomforts will open doors and avenues into His presence formerly closed to the faint at heart. God has to make us bold and courageous where normally we would have fled the scene or sidestepped the issues altogether. God has to design our circumstances to where we are unable to remain passive or exit the 'test' for our own good and the building of our own godly characters.

The yolk is such that we are together harnessed in it with Jesus. When He moves we move, when he turns we turn. When He decides to walk through unfamiliar places that cause us fear and concern we go along with Him: we are tied to Him, with Him.

Believe it or not, this is the ultimate place of rest for our souls. We do not have to carry the weight or pull the load on our own. Nor do we have to know where we are going or how to get there. We are bound together and He is leading. We will be fed and all our needs taken care of.

He is aware of my needs. He knows my pain and wounds as they occur; He is touched with the feelings of my infirmities - how can He not be, we walk so close together. I can just whisper them to Him; I can feel His breath on my face. Even in my dark moments and discouragement, when I feel I can't pull anymore and at times when I just don't want to, He's right there. He knows me well; our shoulders rub together in this journey. He will wait for me. He steadies my impulsiveness as I surrender to my restraints unable to run ahead without leaving the yolk he designed for us. There is only safety, security and life under the yoke of God.

The yoke of God is the Cross of Christ, the place of transforming power of the Gospel. "I have been crucified with Christ; and it is no longer I who live, but Christ lives in me; and the life which I now live in the flesh I live by faith of the Son of God, who loved me, and delivered Himself up for me (Galatians 2:20a).

> "But we are so framed that spiritual greatness may be a snare. It may lead to boasting which is destructive victory which leaves the victor in chains of pride. Our guardian Lord knew this and since it is better to prevent than to heal He touched the hollow of Jacob's thigh and it was out of joint. Here we have a mirror which reflects many of the Lord's dealings with His favored children. In prevailing they are crippled lest by prevailing they should perish.
>
> Strong grace is checked by enfeebled flesh lest it should climb the dizzy heights of self-esteem. Many halting infirmities convince them that a yielding Lord has power to lay low. They learn than victory is His gift and not the wages of their might. They feel that they are broken reeds, except God works with them to will and to do."
> -Henry Law

Chapter 5

Gateway to an Open Heaven

Someone may say this is all true and ok for Jesus, but this cross business and all this talk of suffering is old school; we're living in a new day; we're under grace; we are not anyone's Savior, so why should we even accept a doctrine or teaching that we have to suffer? What will my sufferings or trials do for me?

For all of us who turn to our Bibles as the only authoritative voice of truth, let's take some time to consider a few of a great many scriptures on the believers association to trials, tribulations and suffering and their purpose for the saint of God.

One of the purposes of suffering is that we cease to and refrain from sinning, stop serving our flesh and live to do the will of God. 1 Peter 4:1-2, "Therefore since Christ has suffered in the flesh, arm yourself also with the same purpose, because he who has suffered in the flesh has ceased from sin. so as to live the rest of the time in the flesh no longer for the lusts of men, but the will of God."

Another verse in 1 Peter 4 states, "Beloved do not be surprised at the fiery ordeal among you, which comes upon you for your testing, as though some strange thing were happening to you; but to the degree that you share the sufferings of Christ, keep on rejoicing; so that at the revelation of His glory you may rejoice with exultation" (12-13).

Peter is trying to reassure the believers that suffering is part and parcel of the Christian life so don't be surprised when suffering comes your way; it's not a strange or uncommon thing happening to you. Remember, to whatever degree you suffer keep rejoicing so at the revelation of His glory you will rejoice with exultation, or in other words, you will all be one super excited bunch of Christians.

Bottom line, trials come. Do not get bent out of shape; there is a grace to keep you on the rejoicing side of things. By the way, that term Peter used - "fiery ordeal" - describes a smelting process where intense heat is applied to metal to remove the impurities within it. For us, intense trials become our smelter or fiery furnace to remove the impurities of our own hearts and mind. Tests are a refiner's fire.

To be sure, persecution is certainly a part of the sufferings. There are areas of the world where believer's lives are placed on the altar of supreme sacrifice and they give it all. How do we relate to this type of 'dying to self'? Outside of the enabling grace of God no one can give so much and remain in the joy of the Lord.

In the West today, persecution for one's faith would, in most cases, consist of being told that we (Christians) are narrow minded and naïve. This is not said to diminish the fact that there are still people losing their lives today for their faith. How could we, in a safer area of the world, benefit from trials and sufferings that hardly qualify as persecution?

The cross and path that God has chosen is custom made for each of us. In Mathew 16:24 "Jesus said to His disciples if any one wishes to come after Me, let Him deny himself, take up his cross and follow Me." An honest look at this verse would reveal the idea of forsaking our own way and taking up the cross, renouncing a past way of thinking and doing and literally choosing to terminate a part of our 'self' thinking pattern to embrace His. It is a life with a price tag. We choose His way instead of our way His will in place of our will, His life in exchange of my life!

> The sufferings of the believer have the handprints of God all over them; it does not take some genius detective, following the endless clues, to figure out that God is, as it were, 'guilty' of afflicting His children, either as an accomplice or by His very own hand. Isaiah 53:10, prophetically speaking of Jesus, teaches "But the Lord was pleased to crush Him putting Him to grief." This clearly and undeniably states that God the Father was "pleased". Actually, the word also means that 'He took delight in crushing'; another rendering says 'beat to pieces putting Him to grief or making Jesus weak, sick and afflicted'.

Jesus did not have to guess who was allowing these evil acts to take place. He knew it came from the Father's hand and heart. For the rest of us we have the hardest time thinking and believing God could allow such terrible things to happen to His children.

Yet Jesus was in the will of the Father, right? Now if we are walking in the center of God's known will for us, as much as we can know right now and if we are not running out from under the safety umbrella to go serve or indulge in our own desires for a time, is it so hard to grasp that God might still allow adversity or affliction to hit our campsite? Why would He do that to me, one might ask; well why would He allow Jesus to suffer?

Hebrews 5:7-9 holds a key: "In the days of His flesh, when He offered up both prayers and supplications with loud crying and tears to Him who was able to save Him from death and who was heard because of His piety, although He was a Son, He learned obedience from the things which He suffered; and having been made perfect, He became to all those who obey Him the source of eternal salvation."

Jesus learned obedience from the things which He suffered, and suffering in the Father's will taught Jesus submission and compliance. Obedience wasn't a given; He just couldn't say 'Hey Dad I already know all about that obedience stuff, lets skip that part of the lesson and move on to the miracles'. The only route available and the only means that could bring about the results that verse nine describes as "having been made perfect" (complete or mature) came to Him because He obeyed and submitted Himself to the Fathers cross and the suffering. Can we expect to take the shortcut and end up where God really places the value, which is being made perfect and complete - a mature son of God?

For Jesus to be that Lamb without spot or wrinkle He had to be tempted in all points to really prove what this Son of God was really all about. In 1 Peter 1:7 Peter talks about a faith more precious than gold which is perishable and tried or tested by fire. This test of fire is to remove the impurities in the gold - our faith. The testing of Jesus carried with it eternal stakes and consequences. He could not fake it or just "hang in there".

He went from the stable to the cross and experienced every form of adversity known to man; He had to, the Father made sure of it. Jesus did not live in a bubble on this earth. His childhood was normal: the scrapes and bruises were real. Every thought of temptation, anger and retaliation were all real issues He faced. Rejection from others, the words of accusation, broken friendships and the myriads of circumstances that presented themselves were all felt and they impacted a real human being and not a god.

Our suffering reveals the depth of brokenness and 'yieldedness' to the Lord. We all have different thresholds of how much we can take. God in His goodness provides the way of escape, not to exit the temptation but that we might be able to endure it (1 Cor.10:13).

Today everyone wants the power. We have conferences to teach people how to move in the power of God, how to receive the power of God, and they are all usually well attended. The down side being that, twenty years later, we are all still going to the similar conferences trying to get the latest nine keys to spiritual power. I wonder, if we put on a conference that taught people 'how to embrace their cross' or 'how to surrender your life to Christ', how many would show up. I doubt you would get more than a handful.

> The disciple knows he or she must choose the cross; only through the cross and its deadly work does one emerge in a resurrection life so often quoted and referred to but so rarely manifested in practical ways in the Church.

Could it be possible that we have missed the great secret of moving in the power of God and could it be possible that its source and flow are rooted in a life of brokenness and in a God ordained road of adversity?

This is not the road of complaints and murmurs. This is a Calvary road where the sons and daughters reach into God. Here they are hidden away in the 'secret place of His presence' and learn to draw from that resurrection flow to endure and overcome.

Again, I would emphasize, as Paul did in so many places, the wisdom and power of God through the believers trials. This is not about self-inflicted beatings or some distorted religious view on penance or how to merit God's blessings or favor.

In 2 Corinthians1:3-5 Paul writes, "Blessed be the God and Father of our Lord Jesus, the Father of mercies and God of all comfort; who comforts us in all our afflictions so that we may be able to comfort those who are in any afflictions with the comfort with which we ourselves are comforted by God. For just as the SUFFERINGS (my emphasis) of Christ are ours in abundance so also our comfort is abundant through Christ."

Right in the midst of our trials and adversity we find the Father as an ever present help in time of trouble, ready to comfort us, that we in turn might comfort those who are experiencing their 'dark night of the soul'.

Imagine a time when we as a body of believers will actually begin to deny ourselves, take up our crosses and finally put an end to our seemingly perpetual infancy - a stage we have been so accustomed to, a Biblical milk diet and a Christianity that revolves around us and our needs.

An Outdated Gospel

A Prayer: Father I am tired of this pattern in my life; I feel my life is going nowhere. There is a desire for more of You, yet I don't really know how to come into this intimate 'son ship' relationship. I acknowledge my selfishness and my self-serving ways. I ask for Your forgiveness and in all sincerity that You would begin to transform my life by whatever means You desire. I trust in Your will for me, and I am at rest with the plan You have for me. In Jesus name, Amen.

Chapter 6

Pressed Into Conformity

Song of the Bow, a Song in the Night

The closing chapter in 1 Samuel ends on a very sorrowful note. King Saul, the first king of Israel, is slain on Mount Gilboa along with his sons Jonathan, Abinadab and Malchi-shua. The first chapter of 2 Samuel opens with a man from King Saul's camp breaking the news to David and his men concerning the battle in which Saul and his sons were slain.

Upon hearing the news David took hold of his clothes and tore them, and so did all the men who were with him (2 Sam. 1:11-12). Verse 12 describes the great sorrow that took hold of David: "And they mourned and wept and fasted until evening...."

One would think that this should have been good news to David seeing that the King who spent so much time, energy and resources to kill him was finally dead. Maybe David was mourning Jonathan: the two of them had become close friends and not Saul.

As you read down the chapter starting at verse 19, you come away sensing the true condition of David's heart towards Saul. "The Song of the Bow", in verse 18, is a lament that David chanted over Saul and Jonathan and he told the people that they should teach it to the sons of Judah.

A couple of examples reveal the heart of a warrior who had every right to not only defend himself, but even take revenge, but David would not lift his hand against Saul, because he loved and honored the King.

Verse 19: "Your beauty, O Israel, is slain on your high places." How does a man, chased like a wild animal throughout the countryside, describe his pursuer as the "beauty of Israel"?

Verse 23: "Saul and Jonathan, beloved and pleasant in their life …." These are not the words of a man filled with revenge, anger or bitterness in his heart.

Allow me to relate the story in my own words. David is told that the men from Jabesh-gilead took Saul's body and buried it. Hearing this David sends messengers to these men to tell them that they are blessed of the Lord because they showed this kindness to Saul, and David goes on to let them know that God would show them loving kindness and truth and that David himself would show them goodness because of what they did, in burying Saul's body.

Again, I would re emphasize, these are the words and acts of a man filled with love and respect for his King not those of an enemy. You can hear the sorrow and genuine brokenness in his lament; the loss and confusion as to how this tragedy could even have taken place resonate in his words. The lament, its words, emotion and passion, are the expressions of a eulogy from a beloved friend.

Please bear with me as I set up this word picture. I am trying to capture, as evidence, the words of a man to demonstrate the awesome work of God in David's heart.

> David did not wake up one day with the grace, mercy and the character displayed here in 2 Samuel. In our prayers, we may be guilty of thinking that Godly character was just a quick prayer away or that someone laying their hands on our heads imparting godliness or integrity would do it. Our concepts of God and His kingdom are not always accurate. This is due, once again, to our indoctrination of a quick fix nature that requires little or no effort on our part aside from simply asking or just believing it to be so. This is error on a large scale!

Let us back up a little and review David's entrance into the scene from obscurity. Our first introduction to David is found in 1 Samuel 16. God upbraids Samuel the prophet for his ongoing grieving for King Saul who at this point has been rejected as King by God for his habitual disobedience and self will. God is commissioning Samuel to go to Jesse, the Bethlehemite, because He has selected a King from among His sons.

With great fear of retaliation from Saul, Samuel obeys and heads down to Bethlehem. This is all done, for safety sake, under the guise of a sacrifice. God sets it all up, even the words that Samuel is to use. 1 Samuel 16:2b: "take a heifer with you, and say, I have come to sacrifice to the Lord." At the sacrifice, Jesse and his sons were invited, and as they entered, Samuel was giving them the 'look over'. Again, God is directing the program and Samuel is paying attention: "do not look at the outward appearance or at the height of his stature…" (v.7). Samuel, no doubt a little confused, asks Jesse if these are all of his children? Jesse answers and I will paraphrase: 'well, there is our youngest, he is out tending the sheep; we didn't think to have him here being so young, scrawny and insignificant compared to his other brothers. We just thought there was no possible way he could be the one you're looking for'. 'Go get him, we won't start till then' was the word from Samuel. When David entered the Lord said to Samuel "Arise, anoint him; for this is he."

What a moment that must have been. On one hand we understand the great disappointment the other brothers felt being passed over, but we can't help but cheer for David, the little guy. The underdog is being recognized as a somebody, anointed by the prophet of God to be Israel's next King. What a stellar moment.

In our minds we often put ourselves in others shoes and imagine the exhilaration and excitement David felt as he was anointed before his family and town in that "Kodak" moment (to coin an advertisement of another era). There is no mention of any celebration or fanfare that may have accompanied the sacrifice and the meal.

Two things really stand out as we read the following verses. One is in verse 13b: "and the Spirit of the Lord came mightily upon David from that day forward…." Who wouldn't want that? The second sobering point made in verse 14 reads, "Now the Spirit of the Lord departed from Saul and an evil spirit from the Lord terrorized him" - the consequences of a stubborn rebellious heart. An accumulation of sin and a proud, unrepentant heart disqualified Saul from fulfilling his life course as King of Israel.

Now let me ask you, what was David anointed for? Naturally, we would answer, to be King of course and we would be correct, but this is the obvious reply based on what we already know of the story. Let us stand back a moment and look at David's life from an analytical point of view.

I will ask this question again: what was David anointed for? And let us keep in mind what that word anointed or anointing means. The Hebrew word for anointing or anoint is *masah*, a verb meaning "to anoint, smear, consecrate, the Old Testament's most common use is to indicate a special setting apart for an office or function" (Vines Expository of Biblical Words).

One of the New Testament words for anoint/anointing is the word *chrisma*: a noun meaning "an unguent or an anointing, it was prepared from oil and aromatic herbs. It is used only metaphorically in the New Testament of the Holy Spirit, and it indicates that the Holy One has anointed us to ENABLE (my emphasis) us, the believers to not only possess the knowledge of the truth but to do the work of our ministry" (VEBW).

> As Samuel was pouring out the oil over David's head, God was setting him apart for His own special use, and in the true sense of what was taking place, God was enabling him to do the work of his upcoming calling of Kingship.

Now this does not sound too bad, does it? However, in actuality, David was anointed for agony, misunderstanding, suffering, incredible hardship, failure, isolation and loneliness! The enabling was actually to undergird the young shepherd for the rough road ahead. The young lad, strumming his harp on the mountain slopes was set apart or maybe we could say was set up - a reality of which in his wildest dreams he could never have imagined.

Being personally invited to Saul's palace as the favoured harpist was an honour to be sure, that is, until you find out you are the target for the King's javelin practice. What was at one point a fun ministry suddenly turned to fear, panic and then survival. 'This is not what I thought ministry was supposed to be like. Now I am running for my life; I do not understand. This has to be the devil! How can God be in this; everything is upside down? I am misunderstood, and no matter how I try to correct the matter and bring clarity it just seems to get worse. I'm so confused!'

This is only the beginning of travail for David. The next big event is the confrontation with Goliath. The young, enthusiastic warrior on a mission from his father finds himself on the front lines of battle, not of his design, but God's. He gets there in time to hear the blatant blasphemy booming out of the giant's mouth and across the valley floor. David is beside himself at what Goliath is saying and is shocked that no one steps up to the plate to take away the reproach of Israel as the Philistine further taunts the armies of the living God.

To condense this story somewhat, David, in the enabling power and authority of the Lord, runs towards the giant: there was no timidity in his resolve to settle this matter.

He heard the word of the Lord and stepped into the strength of God as one would put on a garment. In a moment it was over. The giant is dead and headless, the Philistine army is on the run and David initiated a great victory for God. Wow, the festivities begin; everybody is giving David the 'high five' and patting him on the back: it is a great day. David earns the hand of the King's daughter; no taxes for his family and great riches await him. I am sure at one point this is the way it was going to turn out until something was triggered in Saul.

David was taken into Saul's house and did not return to his father's house. He was also placed over the men of war - to be sure a great honor. Suddenly, he is highly respected by all the people including Jonathan, Saul's son.

Another defining moment is at hand. In 1 Samuel 18:6-7, we read that as the army came back from the battle the women came out from all the cities in Israel singing and dancing to greet King Saul with tambourines, musical instruments and with great joy. The woman sang, "Saul has slain his thousands and David his ten thousand." One would think that in the spirit of the moment this saying is very innocent, a spontaneous praise for the warriors and their victory. However, this was not the case in King Saul's mind. In verse 8 we read that "Saul became very angry for this saying displeased him." This should have been as far as this went but he could not get over it. As he pondered the saying, he wrongly concluded that the only next step for David was to take the kingdom from him and thus David's motives are misunderstood and he again finds himself at odds with Saul.

I am sure when David heard the women singing those words he was cringing inside, knowing that Saul was anxious to get back to the basement of the palace to prepare a few more javelins to use against him.

There is another interesting parallel here. Saul is a type or a symbol of a man led only by his natural inclinations. He could be compared to an unbroken stallion just running loose and free to pursue his own ends. He is a natural man, tossed about by each day's events, an emotional roller coaster, ruled by jealousy and insecurity, ready to kill anyone who even appears to take too much responsibility that cuts into his rule: this is Saul.

As bad as that may be, it is still not the worse part. Saul's stubborn self-will led him out of the ordained will and calling of God into the 'judgment zone'. This is the place where the mercy and grace of God appeals to us to return, repent and obey His voice. To continue to head into this 'zone' is like pulling your own switch in the electric chair; it is a really dumb idea, especially when God provides us opportunity to change our minds and mend our ways and get out of the chair. He is not willing that any should perish.

> Can we discern that the Lord is creating in David 'a song in the night' - the orchestrating of events that read like the musical score from a great symphony piece? God is setting David's love in right order and weaning him from his own natural strength and wisdom.

This is a not a song one learns from a music sheet that someone has written from inspiration; this song is 'birthed under' the pressures of our circumstances. This is a place with no outlet and no natural release - a pressure in a confined space. It is the kind of pressure where words cannot be uttered, except maybe, through deep groaning.

This song emerges from within the soul of a child of God as they enter into the wine press of the Lord. This may not sound like the theology you may have been taught, but this is the practical workings of a Father inscribing His identity and image on the hearts of His sons as He takes them along His ways unto maturity.

How do you describe the seasons where God just does not seem to answer our 911 calls? In desperation we cry, we plead, we even get angry and accuse God of being unfair and insensitive along with a whole lot more. In our pain and discomfort, we cry for release and none comes: no one comes to our rescue.

It is our dark side of the moon. Does anyone care or even know what I am going through? Probably not! Unless of course we are so vocal, going around complaining to anyone and everyone about how hard were having it. Unlike the children of Israel, we do need to exercise wisdom about how we respond to Gods dealings with us. The Lord understands our anger and frustration in the midst of our desert places. Our being 'pressed' does bring up the worst in us at times. Our unwillingness to yield or to become hard and defiant may lead to an extension of time being added to our wilderness journey.

This is not to say that we are not free to seek counsel. We have the freedom to share our hearts with others and receive prayer as they agree to stand with us.

There is a possibility that we may have never been taken down that road. Hold on! God proves all of His children eventually; in time, we shall see what we are made of. We may be surprised at what He allows us to see inside our own hearts. We do need to see it though.

> In the process of suffering, after the anger, after the meltdowns and the threats have subsided, when we believe we cannot endure any more and all is laid on the altar, our song is made pure. At some point in the 'night time' of our being pressed out of ourselves, God is pressing or stamping an image that is of the very nature of His Son within us.

It cannot be manufactured or purchased any other way; it is the narrow way that leads to His life. It is the song of sweet incense that ascends to the Father and whispers in His ear the sound of our absolute surrender. This is not a once in a lifetime event; many of us would wish it so. This place will become a familiar place in the purposes of our Father as He Himself meets with us in a process that could only be described as a transfusion of life and essence from our natural makeup to a Christ like composition. A transference from a carnal outlook to a spiritual mindset brought about by intense God ordained pressure.

In studying David's life, I am not so sure that I would want to pay the price David did to get where he did. Nevertheless, our road is not of our own making or design: "the steps of a righteous man are ordered of the Lord" (Proverbs 20:24). We can only choose to walk with God and obey His voice, or we can strike out on our own and face the consequences. We will always be free to make our own choices.

This is not to say that David or any other saint of God is perfect in their faith, their practice, their theology or creeds. The Father's ways supersedes them all. He transcends our denominational affiliations, ties, gender and race.

It is the call itself from the Father that gives us all significance, relevance and purpose, without which it all goes back to nothing more than religious duty and meaningless servitude.

"... but join me in suffering for the gospel according to the power of God, who has saved us and **called** (my emphasis) us with a holy calling, not according to our works, but according to His own purpose and grace which was granted us in Christ Jesus from all eternity..." (2 Timothy 1:8-9).

There is a suffering for the gospel as the messenger works to bring the gospel to others. The suffering may be the plans, preparations, prayers, study and finances. Simultaneously there is a deep work taking place within the messenger. The messenger in time will resemble the One who sent him/her.

It is interesting to look at our word apostle. The Greek rendering for apostle is "one sent forth" having been chosen and appointed by God for a particular office of the church with the vision and authority to establish it firmly to oversee it and expand its dominion on the earth.

We, as believers in like manner, are sent forth in the great commission to the world to bring the good news to every nation, while the Lord is establishing in us His dominion and rule. There is a principle here of life and death happening at the same time within us.

Paul described it this way: "But we have this treasure in earthen vessels, that the surpassing greatness of the power may be of God and not from ourselves; we are afflicted in every way, but not crushed; perplexed but not despairing; persecuted, but not forsaken; struck down, but not destroyed; always carrying about in the body the dying of Jesus, that the life of Jesus also may be manifested in our body" (2 Cor. 4:7).

Just in case we may venture to think that this kind of lifestyle was only for Paul and the great apostles, we read a little later in the same chapter of 2 Corinthians 4:16-17. "Therefore we [we plural, all of us Christians] do not lose heart, but though **our** outer man is decaying, yet **our** inner man is being renewed day by day, for momentary, light affliction is producing for **us** an eternal weight of glory far beyond all comparison" (Emphases mine).

Whoever said that we would dance our way through the kingdom was greatly mistaken. We must allow our thinking to be altered. The negative problems that come our way are not ordered of the devil contrary to popular belief.

Let us remember Paul again, as the Lord reminds him, "my grace is sufficient for you, for power is perfected in weakness." What is Paul's response: 'come on God, enough is enough already, how long do I have to go through these tests? I'm getting sick and tired of it, give me a break!'

That would more aptly describe the attitude of some of us who expect that our lives should maintain this wonderful, smooth flow of beauty, peace and harmony - a world where Christians never experience bad things, where our words are always full of grace and truth, where love flows from our mouths like honey to everyone no matter how wicked they may have acted towards us. Our paradise is one of answered prayers the moment we pray them.

Sound nice, maybe a little unrealistic? There is a message that has taken root in the western gospel that is very similar to this pipe dream syrupy goop. The sad truth being that when the real deal comes along it is oftentimes rejected because it sounds and feels too tough to be God and so the ear ticklers are successful in propagating error as it makes for them a very good living and, to be sure, the hearers want to reap the benefits and not have to experience the adverse circumstances of real Christian living on planet earth.

> This is not to advocate a life-long Christian experience devoid of blessing and Godly favor. This is not about the believer enduring a joyless and dismal existence under the hand of a ruthless dictator. Religion has held the high ground on that kind of practice and thinking too long. I am talking about the narrow road that leads to life; albeit narrow, it is still the road that leads to life.

We do have to choose. It is not the choice between heaven and hell - that was taken care of at our salvation. The choice here is the difference between good and best. It is the upward call of Christ as opposed to settling for the normal or nominal Christian life. It is the difference between spiritual infancy and full-grown Sons.

Our inner man gives witness to a superior way as Paul so accurately points out "for momentary light affliction is producing **for us** (my emphasis) an eternal weight of glory far beyond all comparison" (1 Corinthians 10:11). I believe compared to the saints of old and the New Testament believers we are going through even lighter afflictions than what they suffered. Perspective is everything. In hindsight, we have the added benefit of seeing what they went through and how they acted and reacted as a lesson for how we should live.

Tell me if this verse takes on a new meaning in light of what I have been talking about: "But whatever things were gain to me, those things I've counted as loss for the sake of Christ. More than that, I count all things loss in view of the surpassing value of knowing Christ Jesus my Lord, for whom I have suffered the loss of all things, and count them but rubbish in order that I might gain Christ" (Philippians 3:7-8). This is the testimony of someone who forsook a great deal to gain Christ - the ultimate possession. He understood the cost and paid it.

Now back to David for a moment. In Psalms 142 we catch a glimpse of one of the many dark sides of the moon he lived through. This particular Psalm is earmarked "prayer for help in trouble". This Psalm describes the time when David was being pursued by King Saul and had hidden himself in a cave. Remember he is the anointed of the Lord.

> Psalm 142:
> "I cry aloud with my voice to the Lord; I make supplication with my voice to the Lord. I pour out my complaint before Him; I declare my trouble before Him. When my spirit was overwhelmed within me, Thou didst know my path. In the way where I walk they have hidden a trap for me. Look to the right and see; for there is no one who regards me; there is no escape for me; No one cares for my

soul. I cried out to Thee, O Lord; I said" Thou art my refuge, my portion in the land of the living. Give heed to my cry, for I am brought very low; deliver me from my persecutors, for they are too strong for me. Bring my soul out of prison, so that I may give thanks to Thy Name; The righteous will surround me. For Thou will deal bountifully with me."

This is no walk in the park with his friends. This is a man in trouble and he knows it, but he also knows the One who can sustain him and deliver him.

> We often fear that we will be put in situations where we have no control, and so the idea for us to just surrender our lives to God is not very appealing to our flesh. The Bible accounts that we read about can leave us with an uneasy feeling of not wanting to even consider the option of a God completely in charge, and I mean completely in charge: it is just too risky. Is it any wonder why we only see very limited manifestations of God's power in our lives or churches? Our grip is just too tight!

David was in the cave overwhelmed, trapped and without escape, but even in this dilemma, he was completely in the palm of God's hand.

Fear, is enemy number one for the Christian. Given a foothold, it begins to reach into our understanding of God like the tentacles of a terrible octopus, choking out any hope for our future. Fear is also like an opaque veil which begins to conceal the testimony of God's goodness of our past; it also blinds us to God's present help to bless, deliver and to be strong on our behalf. We are left feeling weak, powerless and unable to change any of our circumstances; whatever faith is left cannot even rise high enough to touch the ceiling.

The voice we hear wants to place the last nail in our coffin by telling us God will not hear our prayer: we have sunk too low. That voice continues to try to persuade us that God is disappointed with us. We are an embarrassment to the church; we may as well throw in the towel and leave quietly out the back door. Don't even bother anyone for prayer; you're not worth the time or effort. It is the same old tactics, but they work well on us. The devil just keeps doing us in; he is good at his craft.

The reassuring part in this equation is that we have a faithful God. He never leaves town on us. The purpose for our testing is not so God may find something on us that was hidden deep down only to expose our shame and let us squirm around trying to cover our sense of nakedness. He has enough goods on us if embarrassing us was actually His prime motivator to get us to co-operate like some kind of spiritual blackmail. Imagine, if God is trying to take us to a higher place in Him, would He say, 'do this now, or else all the angels of heaven will be sent to your church and neighborhood and announce your darkest sin!' No! He is not like that and thank you Lord You are not!

Whether it's David being chased around the countryside by a jealous King, or facing the uprising of his own son Absalom who is out to overthrow David's kingdom. How about the capture of his family and those of his men by the Amalekites, and if that wasn't hard enough to take at that moment, his own men spoke of stoning David out of their misplaced grief and anger. How would any of us pull through some of those adversities with our resolve to love and honor God still intact? In our own distress and dismay we would have been spiraling down in no time.

However, here is the key. If we want to reign and understand the authority of God then that, which is so unlike God must be replaced with that which is like Him. God is looking for more than just anointing someone to do a great work; even donkeys can be anointed to speak as in the case of Balaam. Our testimony, character and integrity will require some iron to be mixed into our souls.

> The hand of God tested David and the instrument used was Saul. King Saul, in essence, was the smith that purged the very nature of David's heart. David, like all of us, had the potential to become like Saul. We all by nature are children of wrath (Ephesians 2:3) and by that nature produce its fruit: selfish, ruthless, jealous, angry, self-serving and on and on.

I believe and the Bible bears record that God, on several occasions, tried to rein in King Saul. It was not God's plan to have a practice run in which Saul never really had a chance at truly reigning over the nation. On the contrary, God wanted to establish the kingdom for him and his sons after him. Yet after several defiant acts of disobedience, the kingdom was removed and given to David. Even at this point; had Saul obeyed and humbled himself, his demise and legacy could have been very different.

King of Israel number two – David - was not about to walk into the palace and sit on the throne. God had boot camp planned for this shepherd boy. Any dreams he may have had about his coronation with all its pomp and ceremony were not about to happen for quite some time.

Please hear me, all of us have grandiose plans on how we will serve the Lord as great men and woman for God and we are sincere in our desire to do and to be somebody for God. But the truth of the matter is that, like King Saul, we have no idea what is on the inside of us waiting to potentially abort our gift or ministry. Does that mean we all have to be perfect for God to use us? Not at all; I think we have it backwards many times. We all want to go on in God to do wonderful things and see people being blessed, healed and set free, and yes God has appointed us all to do the work of the ministry (Ephesians 4: 11-13), and it's great to be a part of what the Holy Spirit is doing and being able to work along with Him.

In the midst of all this activity of doing, the Father is seeking those who want to become. The mindset of servants of the Lord revolves around doing things for God. This is commendable; we will always serve in some capacity. Serving brings great joy to the Lord and fulfillment in the servant's heart. There is the satisfaction of accomplishing the work in the kingdom, the sense of purpose, and seeing great things happen in the lives of others: it is all good.

However, the mindset of the Son or Daughter is different: 'Yes Father I delight in all those wonderful things you are allowing me to do, to see them and take part in them. It is so fulfilling and yet why do I feel something is still missing. Father, I just do not want a blessing and an anointing; I want the inheritance of the children of God. I not only want to do for you but I want to be like You; I want to see You as You are that I may be as You are (1 John 3:2-3). Nothing else will satisfy my soul.'

> Servants will always serve and be content to remain in the 'outer courts'. Sons however, serve and become the full heirs of God's provision. Servants are not brought in to that inner circle of fellowship; the Sons are processed into it. This is more than just a birth issue, for we who are born again have all been born of God. The difference being many are satisfied with outer court servitude: trim the lamps, bring the wood for the sacrifice, bring the sacrifice, etc. And please hear me, servants do a great job of it.

What I point to as a sterling example is our Old Testament Joshua. He had the habit of slipping into the "Tent of Meeting" where Moses was meeting with God. Joshua's obvious thirst for more of God consisted in staying back after Moses left and absorbing every residue of God's glory. I am sure he cultivated his own relationship as he tarried there (Exodus 33:11). This is about not being satisfied - in a good way - with the depth and experience of our relationship with the Father.

Another reference is found in Exodus 33:7 and it describes how Moses pitched a tent outside the camp a good distance away for anyone who sought the Lord. They had to go outside the familiar place of the camp and enter in on their own without Moses. In the isolation of that tent, they had the privilege to enter into something completely new for these former slaves: His Presence.

Even Moses, whom the Lord used to lead his people out of Egypt with miracle signs and wonders, still cried out from the depths of his heart "I pray Thee, show me Thy glory." The 'doing' even of miraculous things will never satisfy the deep longing of our hearts, until we see Him, and that's not about waiting until heaven (John 14:21-23).

So then, the Moses' and the David's, the Josephs and the Daniels seemed to have looked beyond the season of their life and observed, as if with a telescope, a place of abiding in God not yet even written about. Not satisfied with only the blessing of doing the works of the kingdom, but of being true sons in position to receive the inheritance, the full download from the Father. They pray 'Lord let me see You, let Your glory pass by in front of me I pray' (Exodus33:18-23).

In response the Father unearths the heart of each of His 'sons' like a grave full of rot and decay. He reaches into the putrid mass to touch the unclean, foul condition of our souls. Thus, He begins the process of restoration, life and transformation, calling into being those things which are not from the chaos within, and creating life, order and eternal purpose.

Every child of God born to Him is set aside to become the full-grown mature child who receives their full inheritance. Our hearts cry at every turn must be 'search me O God; let me know the condition of my heart; keep me from deceiving myself into thinking that I can side-step your searchlight and conviction and still remain in close fellowship with you. I know You want nothing more than to bless my going out and coming in, but I pray that even those blessings never interfere with your utmost eternal plan for me: conforming me to Christ.'

Finally, we will close this chapter with a few verses from Psalms 51:

> "Create in me a clean heart, O God, and renew a steadfast spirit within me.
>
> Do not cast me away from Thy presence, and do not take thy Holy Spirit from me. Restore unto me the

joy of thy salvation, and sustain me with a willing spirit" (10-12).

How refreshing to hear no excuses or blame as the Lord puts His finger on David's heart and out of its depth comes true sorrow and brokenness. David had sinned to the degree that some of us might find to be off the chart. He does hide his sin for close to a year, but when God sends a prophet to confront him **David is broken**.

This Psalm is the reflection of a man apprehended by the goodness and the mercies of his God; his only concern is his relationship with God, not his **throne**.

We began this chapter with David's lament for Saul and Jonathan. He is still a fugitive at this point, his crown still to come, and even after so many hardships he was still to face many more. Some because of wrong choices, some were simply the full-born fruit of past mistakes in family relationships coming home to roost. For whatever reasons, we, like David, will face the harvest of our planting - good or bad. The defining line that will mark us will be the response of our hearts in the midst of our crises.

> David's song in the night under the pressure of his adversity was free from the bitterness of his suffering. Any gall that could have been produced in him had been pressed out of him. What came forth, even upon hearing the tragedy of Saul, was a song of love and honour to a beloved King and not an enemy. The winepress of his suffering had created the song. It was a sound unknown to the natural man. God plucked at the strings of David's heart and played the song birthed in the travail of his dark nights.

It was the Father's favorite song, the same sound that came from the mouth of Jesus on the cross: "Father forgive them, they know not what they do" (Luke 23:34). David had truly become a King, but more importantly, a Son of God.

Chapter 7

I Did It My Way

For many of us Christians our lives are well packaged, planned and controlled. We all want more of God, but we really do not want Him upsetting our apple cart. We feel our lives are boring and uneventful, yet we still hold on to the reins tightly. The thought of getting radical for God is like unchartered waters; there is this inner spiritual Christopher Columbus inside of us that yearns to launch out into the deep things of God. It is a desire to sound out spiritual depths and explore unknown shores that quite possibly would open up spiritual dimensions never imagined.

Then there is the lawyer within us as well always raising the 'what if's', and so we hesitate and we wait for more favourable winds to blow, and before long we have reasoned ourselves past another 'window' of God's visitation. The window was a moment or a season of time where our hearts were tender before Him and the circumstances seem to dictate that certainly a change was not only in order but also greatly desired and needed.

Israel has a history of missing the moment of God for their nation and people. The most striking is where Jesus Himself, in Luke 19:43-44, is actually speaking prophetically of future events for the nation, and yet sadly, also of judgment: "For the days will come upon you when your enemies will throw a bank before you, and surround you and hem you in on every side, and will level you to the ground and your children within you, and they will not leave within you one stone upon another, because you did not recognize the time of your visitation."

> A sobering pronouncement over His people and nation: they had missed Him! A people with a rich spiritual heritage, a history of great men and woman of faith, teachers and scribes passionate for their religion, customs and doctrines, all looking back or looking forward, but only few, very few, could see before them the present Incarnate Son of God.

Why are we here and what are we doing in light of God's eternal purpose for us now? The history of the Jewish faith is not only part of our spiritual history; it is also a parallel to ours as Christians. Call it human nature, but we as a people just seem to fall into old familiar patterns. Our religion makes us religious, and that is not meant to be a compliment.

For all of us who, before we came into a personal relationship with Jesus Christ, or before we were saved, belonged to some mainline religion, let's go back and take an honest look at the condition of our thought life, our attitudes and general outlook as a religious person. A very small percentage might say 'my faith was real; I truly loved God and obeyed Him out of a pure heart desiring to do His will.' The rest of us would fall into the category of 'I did what was necessary to be a member of my particular church brand, and even that would be stretching the truth somewhat.'

Our religious past, if we have one, was made up of a whole lot of tradition, ceremony, ritual and little of God. We were sure proud of our denominations and more often than not we may have liked to think of ourselves as a 'cut above the rest'. We had the corner on truth; our ancestors who built the church and wrote our songs were real pillars, in fact, their names are still written on the base of the pillars at the front of the building.

Let's face it; we were proud of our religious life even though our hearts were not in it. There was no passion for God and His laws and precepts were a great idea for the heathen, but somehow we were able to get ourselves around the 'thou shalt nots'.

> It was not a part of us; it was strictly a garment we wore on the outside. We were very different on the inside. Some would call it play acting, a façade, pretense; I think God would call it hypocrisy. Honestly, we felt we did not need to practice that stuff, and those who did practice it were not very good at it either, and so it was hard to distinguish between those who worked hard at religion and those who didn't really try. It seems we all hung out at the same places, and the church was not one of them. No one could tell us apart by what we did or what we said. Honestly, what was the difference?

There is an old saying that says "you can take the boy out of the bathroom, but you can't take the bathroom out of the boy", or in Christian lingo it might sound like this 'you can take the man out of Egypt, but you can't take Egypt out of the man.' We will never come into the things of God wearing the garment of the world with the attitude of the world. Our spirituality must surpass our role-playing and pretenses. Our old traditional forms may have been left behind and we may have been born again into the kingdom, but if we decided to sit down, tarry and take pride in the fact that we arrived, we are shortchanging ourselves on a grand scale.

There is a chance that we may have only exchanged **garments**. Mind you the point I'm making is not about the sincerity of our salvation; the question is do we have a spiritual appetite or is the pattern of weekly church visits enough to satisfy our religious needs?

Jesus looked over Jerusalem and lamented. They had it all: the history, the prophets, the teachers of the law, the temple and the sacrifice all handed down to them by their forefathers who received it from God Himself. The sad irony is that the very teachings that were handed down and taught to them from children were now pointing to Jesus Himself who was the embodiment of all the laws and prophets (Gal. 3:24).

The Son of God was in their midst, teaching them, and working great miracles and they did not recognize Him: how tragic. Day after day, week after week, Jesus taught in the temple, worked miracles among the large crowds of followers and yet the most anointed and gifted teacher and prophet ever to set foot on the planet could not get the truth through to them about who He was. His teachings, although enthusiastically received failed to penetrate the hearts of most; the appeals fell on deaf ears as He pleaded with many to believe in Who He was. The Jewish leaders were infuriated many times when Jesus publicly corrected them to try and crack the hardened religious shell, but to no avail.

Their systems were so ingrained into them; tradition of religious life beyond question! Truth, especially truth uttered from the mouth of the Son of God must have stirred the Pharisees to their very core. The envy that boiled over so often and was so apparent to all, that in the end carried the nation led by the blind jealousy of its leaders to kill the Holy Messenger and plunge itself to an untimely judgment.

Are we so really different than the leaders of that day? We hear so often about the desire of God that we should be one. Unity of the believers: that is where God command's the blessing (Psalm 133). The fact is we are in no hurry to open up the coffers of our church bank account and (without any strings attached) bless the struggling church or pastor down the road or across the street in our town or city. We tend to be like the birds: we flock together with those who are of the same feather. There is an inconsistency in us all - a disconnect between our words and our deeds.

> Have we begun to take pride in the structures of what we have built and of who we are and what we have? Yet realistically, we have no substance, at least none to speak of. The occasional move of God in the western church in the form of "revivals" seems to bring out the worst in us Christians in the form of mean spirited attacks, accusations of every dimension, much of it motivated by the same envy that hounded Jesus and Paul in their ministries.

Who is that individual who is willing to cross those well-defined lines and risk the wrath and vitriol of their peers, to take the hand of other church leaders and members and just love them and genuinely care for them? We do it for the lost, but hardly for other churches. We tell ourselves: 'well if they can't pull through it's because God is not blessing them and if He isn't blessing them why should we?' It is so true, we Christians bury our wounded, and we don't wait till there dead.

I have said all this to say: we need to desperately rethink the way we do church. Our ideas of what constitutes success may be at odds with God's idea. God is after something in us and until He has it, we will wander around enjoying some measure of blessing and favour, tracing our pattern of doing things on the blueprint of the world and reaping limited benefits, very limited.

What is God after more than anything else? Our obedience! I know this is not the greatest revelation you may have ever heard, but it's one of the greatest truths we can ever know. This fact alone reveals the true attitude of our hearts and reveals how much of God and His kingdom will be entrusted to us by the Father.

Remember in Hebrews 5:8: "although He was a Son, He learned obedience from the things He suffered." The obedience is what He learned by having to suffer. He ultimately died on the cross, but Jesus carried a cross daily. His will was surrendered daily to the Father, only one will emerged - the Fathers. Out of His obedience, the Father released the unrestricted flow of His authority; it was not a given even though He was the Son. It is not enough for us to mouth the nice prayers of surrender and consecration. God will certainly allow His word and His ways to try us and weigh us; our substance will be put to the test. Are we simply a vessel with only a form and structure? Or do we have life giving substance to share with others that we've obtained in the secret place of obedience.

In God's love, we shall be tried repeatedly so that we might see our true inner intentions as He Himself sees us, not to condemn but to correct, change and build us up. It's a painful process, the reality of our confession is being brought into line with whom God is fashioning us to become on the inside.

> What prevents us from becoming all that God would have us to be? Our own undisciplined and independent selves. Our indoctrination of so many worldly and religious attitudes and mindsets that have lodged themselves in our thought processes are very much at home in us and continue to exert their influence on our thinking and outlook and still remain undetected for the most part. Relying on ourselves and our devices to advance God's work and His kingdom in this earth is futility.

Like Samuel we are oftentimes looking for the bigger and the better and though we may say different, we continue to look for that which will attract the crowds: the drawing card or big name to pull people in or to keep us in and happy. Could we receive from some untitled person in the way of correction or teaching or does it have to be a religious celebrity or prophet so-and-so, because he or she will always have a favourable word for me and of course they hear from God.

Now I am certainly not saying that receiving from our own leadership or other recognized ministry is wrong or off and that to receive from some lone ranger walking into the church is somehow more spiritual. Not at all, I'm trying to get at the attitude of our hearts in the way we view people and how we receive and hear the voice of God. If we have it in our minds it can only be one way, we will miss God on a regular basis.

Does He not say in His word that He has chosen the foolish things to shame the wise and the weak things to shame the things that are strong (1 Corinthians 1:27)? He has to break down our own preconceived ideas of how He speaks and how He works and replace them, not with a set pattern but with a listening ear that has learned to put no confidence in self or in our great plans. The patient, listening heart that has learned to wait for the word will walk with a confidence not in themselves but in the 'empowering' that was wrapped and intertwined with the word that heaven sent them. The enablement comes with the marching orders of the day. We do not need an anointing to brush our teeth.

One of the great one-line verses in the Bible that literally speaks volumes, in my opinion anyway, is found in Psalms 103:7: "He made known His ways to Moses, His acts to the sons of Israel." It is easy to read over this without catching the large distinction between "His ways" and "His acts". God made known His ways: what does this really mean and how much different is it than His acts?

The word "ways" in Hebrew is the word *derek*. It means "a road, a course of life, a journey, path a mode of action".

The word "acts" in Hebrew is the word *al ee law, al ee law*. It means "exploits, performance, deeds, doings, inventions and work". (Vines)

I believe the key to understanding this verse is found in the phrase "made known" which is the Hebrew word *yada*. Here are a few of its meanings: "to know, to ascertain by seeing; observation, recognition" and another that compliments this verse is the phrase "privy to": "participating in the knowledge of something private or secret" (www.dictionary.com).

So God made known to Moses His ways, His paths, course of life and mode of His actions. How did He make it known to Moses? We could say Moses was privy to it. Moses was brought in the inner circle if you will. God handpicked Moses and chose to reveal to him, His personal ways.

> His "paths" really speak, not of a destination or route, although it could encompass these aspects, but more of someone who came to know the mind of God and how He did things. Moses was clued in because his heart was fixed towards God and not in any way was it a front or simply lip service. Though God revealed to Moses His ways, Moses needed to learn the process of a close relationship.

With Moses on board, God had a man that He could depend upon to lead a stubborn, rebellious people through a desert for forty years and come out at the other end still intact as a man of God.

Think about this for a moment: you're given a forty year desert sentence for the sins of others! Imagine how he must have suffered. Think of all the confrontations he faced with the people, all the anger unleashed at him, the accusations against him from the other leaders who thought he took too much upon himself as a leader. It was a continuous drama being played out on the desert sands.

Most of the time, Moses and Aaron were on their faces before God and before the rebels. A very humbling place and a most vulnerable place to be as a leader, yet it reveals that Moses had truly learned the source of his strength. Lying down on your face at the next meeting where the angry mob is about ready to string anybody up is not the preferred position we would take. We would most likely bring our own little army of supporters who would be there with us as protection should things get out of hand.

Moses **knew** his God. He was okay on his face; he totally trusted his God for the outcome of every issue that came up. Moses understood God's mode of actions; Moses knew the ways of God.

It is one thing to be chosen by God to do some great work for Him, it is another to maintain a condition of heart that remains pliable and tender towards God when the apple cart is flipped over and the obstacles in our path seem to be overwhelmingly scattered everywhere.

> Keep in mind that the trials have come to test us, no matter how demonic they may appear to be. They have still been filtered through the hands of our Heavenly Father, unless of course, we are out on our own mission outside the umbrella protection of God and we are bent on doing our own thing. Yet, even here we have all experienced the protective mercies of God while doing our own thing.

Just for a moment let's take a look at Samson in contrast: a man called of God to be a judge in Israel over his people. Reading through the chapters in Judges we begin to see a pattern in Samson that is very disturbing. He is a Nazirite who has been set apart for God's purposes from birth, one who has taken vows to live wholly unto the Lord, and yet in his later years we see him on a self-serving, destructive path.

He becomes more acquainted with the harlot's ways than with the ways of his God. We see him lash out at the Philistines in petty anger and revenge, while at the same time God was seeking occasion through Samson to execute judgment on that nation. Sadly, we do not read anything about Samson's devotional life, or of any altars he may have built to mark a place of meeting or of consecration to God. Rather we see a man who did not allow the harness of God or His laws to restrain his passions and therefore ran headlong into a life of self-gratification.

The anointing power of God manifested in a person who has not known the yoke of God's tempering and restraint will not be able to bridle his or her own egos and passions and thus will fall into the same trap as Samson.

We have to keep in mind the purpose for an unction, anointing or ministry.

The seasons of the desert are to prove the heart, to reveal the carnal self-motivated ambitious tendencies, transform and yoke the vessel, to prepare them to receive more, to do more with more, but not for self-serving ends like Samson but to exalt the Lord.

The anointing of God can be very seductive. One senses the enabling power of God and their inner man is quickened by something beyond themselves. A person can begin to move in a realm of the spirit that can often overload the natural mind. This download from heaven opens the door to miraculous things; God's spirit simultaneously imparting wisdom and truth, with prophetic utterances, words of knowledge and in all of this, we may start to believe that we are really something for God to use us in such a powerful manner. Wrong!

However, this is so often the devil's snare to puff us up in pride and then pull the rug out from underneath our feet. God has to highlight and then deal with the deep issues of our heart so that we also may become convinced of our own petty and shallow natural dispositions. He already knows that we have nothing of any substance to offer people within ourselves. Our abiding place of safety is not 'what' we have come to know but Who we know. This statement is not meant to be a slam against our self —esteem; it is an honest appraisal of who we are and what we can and cannot do apart from God.

In the closing chapter of Samson's story we read, "he did not know that the Lord had departed from him" (Judges 16:20). This is a tragic statement. One who was so anointed, strong and mightily used of God, ended up on the knees of Delilah, powerless and oblivious to the fact that God had left him.

Samson's ties to the world became the noose that eventually choked the life of God from him. He was left blind, shaven of his identity as a Nazirite and chained to a milling stone to grind grain for his enemies.

> Our problems cannot be dealt with until they are exposed. God will want to do it in the privacy of our relationship with Him, but if we continue to sidestep the issues at hand we may put off the correction for a while, but our Father will deal with us if we wish to remain His Sons. I think we would all rather be dealt with in the secret place than to be exposed in the public place.

There is enough ground in all of us for the enemy of our souls to plant seeds of pride and self-attainment with the intent to lead us to destruction and cause great damage to others, the church and to the kingdom. Our one focus as a vessel of God is exactly that: that we are only vessels in the hand of the Master.

To remain humble, broken and pliable is quite often not an easy task. We may begin to believe our own press. What are others saying about you, all the compliments the glowing testimonies, the anointing, gifts and fruit coming forth from this man or woman of God? If we are not careful and forget to pass along the praise to Whom it is really due, and if we forget to thank Him for showing up in our ministry and meetings, there is a chance we may start to think we are the men and woman of power for the hour. The North American issue in the church is the same one out in the mainstream world.

So out to the desert we go to unlearn the 'I Did It My Way' attitude and learn the Lord's ways.

The fact remains: we see and hear of ministers and churches going off in their teaching or how some just become bigger than life for all the wrong reasons. Isn't this reason enough for all of us who want to serve God and to be used by Him powerfully and would never want to bring reproach on His name or the church to allow Him unrestrained access to our inner sanctuary where the real you and I reside?

How can we really know ourselves and what we are capable of doing under extreme pressure and temptation? We cannot, and on the other hand do we really know what we will be like when the Spirit of God begins to move through us powerfully and success is the mark of our life and ministry?

Will we have learned along the way that we are men and woman under someone greater than ourselves, where our absolute obedience is essential for our future favor and blessing? Will we be able to say like Jesus, "I only do those things I see my Father do and I only say those things I hear my Father say"?

Let us be honest; this is hard to do even in our everyday natural life. How much more difficult will it be to acknowledge God when we've experienced degrees of success and we've become familiar with the things of God to the point that we are just so sure what His next step would be? In some particular area, we may not know the mind of God, and the danger here is to assume that we know God's direction based on past experience or similar circumstances. God may have moved on and we are still basing our decisions or choices on past experiences and not the present voice of the Holy Spirit.

We may justify it as King Saul did when he began the sacrifice which was not his to do but Samuel the priest. In Saul's mind, the people were dispersing and heading home, leaving the battle scene and him behind. In his assessment, Saul just wanted to get the sacrifice started and keep the people there. Harmless, good intentions right? In our way of thinking, no big deal.

This act along with a few others like it cost Saul his kingdom and favor with God. He had disobeyed repeatedly. Indeed, everyone may be waiting for me to do something or say something; the pressure may be on us to move out before we may have heard the instructions for the moment or situation.

If you have ever done this, you know that disaster is waiting or least an embarrassing moment. This will be a great object lesson for God to teach us about waiting on Him. This is going to hurt, but we will survive to tell about it.

> There is in the life of Jesus, as you read the Gospels, a paramount principle that is stated from His own mouth but is seen over and over again and it's the fact that Jesus is a man under divine authority. He is not free to guess His way through the circumstances all around Him. He is in constant prayer and walking about in an acknowledge-God-mode in every situation. He knows the ways of God because He lives in the ongoing, abiding place of the Father's presence.

Like Moses, he was 'privy to' because he abided in the Lord and from the proximity of his spiritual gaze, recognized and learned the Fathers ways.

Chapter 8

On the Desert Floor

Learning God's Ways

The children of Israel are such a mirror to us; they are our object lesson in many ways (1 Cor. 10: 13). We tend to think that the main issue with them was their constant grumbling and complaining, but that is only a part of the much larger internal issue: the issue of the heart.

1 Corinthians 10:6 is a key verse: "Now these things were our examples, to the intent we should not lust after evil things, as they also lusted." Again, let us look to the Greek for some insight to the original meaning of "should not lust after" (King James Version).

Here we find three Greek words with a lot of punch:
- First word, *einai*: to exist, to be, am, are;
- Second word, *me*: a primary particle of qualified negation, not, never, none;
- Third word, *epithumetes*: a craver, to lust after;

When we put this verse together with an amplified meaning of those words in Greek, verse 6 looks like this: 'Now these things happened as a pattern, example, a model for us that we do not exist to be cravers lusting after worthless depraved things that are injurious to us as they lusted and set their hearts upon them.'

> What is interesting here is that this is a lifestyle, an ongoing pattern that's been die-casted in their minds. We are warned not to take on the same impression or casting as they had. This part of the verse has a familiar ring to it.

Romans 12:2 reads, "and do not be conformed to this world but be transformed by the renewing of your mind that you may prove what the will of God is, that which is good and acceptable and perfect will of God." Simply stated, do not be patterned or fashioned as in a casting or mold but be transformed by having your mind renewed. Don't let the world mold you in its own resemblance!

In our case, we could say do not let their (children of Israel) pattern leave its mark on you that you should follow their bad example. The only way to do this is by having our minds renewed. Out with our own stinking thinking and in with the transforming word of God.

What was it about the children of Israel that they just did not get it? Could it be they just did not want to! As we read on in chapter 10 we find out that they all passed through the sea, all were baptized in Moses and they all ate the same spiritual food. All drank the same spiritual drink - the rock that was Christ - nevertheless, God was not pleased with most of them. Then we read the down side of their wilderness experience:

Do not be idolaters as some of them...
Nor let us act immorally as some of them...
Nor let us try the Lord as some of them...
Nor grumble as some of them...

The result of their actions was judgment, the outcome being, most died (1 Corinthians 10:6-11).

The children of Israel knew His acts. Many times as I have read the story of the Exodus account and the entry into the Promised Land I shake my head and think: how can anybody be so stupid!

Years later, as I've grown and matured somewhat and have seen not only my own but the full grown obstinate fruit of other believers who continue to circle the mountain complaining as they go, not having grasped the lesson of Gods ways, I realize, wow, how very similar we are to them.

How many great and awesome things we have witnessed God do, not only for us but for so many we know. We ourselves were in bondage in a different kind of Egypt but just as real. We were slaves of sins that held us as prisoner; we were unable to free ourselves. Somehow, we knew there just had to be more of life somewhere.

> Our Egypt had conformed us to its ways, its teachings and philosophy - all things it deemed important. All that did not fit Egypt's required pattern was scoffed at, ignored or ruthlessly attacked. Egypt was not about to let its captives go free. We were convinced that Egypt offered everything anyone could ever want or desire, at least that was the intent of the Pharaoh of our Egypt.

The media releases were of a controlled sort, each release was intended to keep us focused on our carnal needs; they were purposed to arouse and awaken our passions, greed and lusts for more. We were convinced we never had enough and more of the same would eventually satisfy the deep needs inside of us.

As slaves, we longed to be free, free from the day to day drudgery of an existence that seemed to go nowhere and left us all feeling empty and purposeless. Being a skilled slave meant some of us were promoted to places of greater power and responsibility which the others envied; this privilege allowed us to eat better and enjoy the nicer things Egypt had to offer, but we still were unhappy. Something was missing; we did not know what.

Pharaoh's slaves resigned themselves to the sobering reality that none escape and all are doomed to spend the rest of their lives in servitude to this Dark Ruler. When it seemed that nothing would ever change and our cries faded into the night skies, God in His mercy sent us our deliverer, Jesus Christ. Like Moses of old, He who was stronger took the captives and led them out of their bondage with great celebration and rejoicing. We were free at last, out of Egypt.

It seemed that the children of Israel, for the most part, were quite content to enjoy the fruits and benefits of their newfound freedom. However, it was not long before these emancipated slaves came face to face with another aspect of their deliverer God.

The mighty I Am, who thunders from the mountaintops and turns the sea blood red is also the God of order. The Creator of the whole universe who stretches out the heavens like a great veil and then takes note when a sparrow falls to the ground was beginning to reveal another aspect of His nature. The God who delivered His people from the bondage of Egypt is also a Father, our Father.

There is just a different ring to Father in contrast to Creator or Deliverer. Our personal connection is made as we respond to Him as Father - a relationship that we all hopefully have found to be a positive one.

> Many I know have struggled with the image of a good and caring heavenly Father because their experience with their own earthly father was rather negative. This however, does not negate the fact that our God is a good and caring Father, tender and sensitive to our innermost needs. Just think of the best Dad we've ever known and then take all the best attributes of other Dads and combine them all into one person and we begin to get a glimpse of the true, genuine goodness of our Father.

Having been in bondage as a nation for over four hundred years, and then to suddenly be set free brings up a picture of a calf in spring time loosed into the corral after a long winter of being boxed in - legs flailing in every direction, turning on a dime and bolting in the opposite direction. You get the picture: abounding energy exploding in the barnyard!

An Outdated Gospel

The Exodus picture is somewhat similar. A conservative estimate of all the people coming out of Egypt would put them at roughly two and a half to three million. Just think for a moment of all that harnessed energy, frustration and anger but also excitement and jubilation all released simultaneously: it is the ultimate emotional roller coaster ride.

Men, woman and children who were under the lash, being told what to do night and day: when to eat, what to eat, the constant threat of death hanging over their head if they disobeyed or displayed any defiant behavior were suddenly free to decide all of these things for themselves. How had they coped all along with the pain of seeing friends or family beat up or killed for not being quick enough to respond to their masters, or having children taken away from parents to be the personal slaves of Egyptians? It was a tragic reality that they may never see them again, to live with the thought that their children were being abused by their captors: this was their day-to-day reality as slaves, and now it was over. A new day had dawned.

What that day looked like and sounded like as they cleared the outskirts of Egypt's territory is not recorded. Behind them, the giant stone images of the Pharaohs', the Pyramids - all reminders of their cruel toil. Being in their sandals at that point must have been surreal, dreamlike. No more sounds of the lash or the barking of cruel soldiers; the only sounds were of singing and nervous laughter pressing forward intent on putting a lot more distance between Egypt and themselves.

Now here they are at the Red sea and the first crisis is unfolding. The Egyptians realized what a mistake they made by letting their workforce go free; Pharaoh hardened his heart again and decided to chase them down and bring them all back. When the children of Israel saw the armies they had a meltdown. They lost all their whit's and the accusations started flying.

You would think that having watched this mighty God completely pull down Egypt and destroy its might and wealth with miraculous wonders would have been proof enough of God's power. Moses rose up and exclaimed, "do not fear, stand by and see the salvation of the Lord which He will accomplish for you today; for the Egyptians you have seen today, you will never see them again forever."

This bold statement of faith came on the heels of some searing accusations that must have pierced Moses heart like a sword: "Is it because there were no graves in Egypt that you have taken us away to die in the wilderness?" If that wasn't enough they further said, "is this not the word we spoke to you in Egypt saying leave us alone that we may serve the Egyptians, for it would have been better for us to serve the Egyptians than to die in the wilderness."

Wow! They wanted to be free but at the first sign of conflict they wanted out of the Exodus plan. In fact, they were now saying that they really did not want to leave in the first place.

So God parts the Red Sea, delivers His people once again and destroys Egypt's finest army by closing the sea over them.

Without going through the whole story, it suffices to say that this was not going to be the picnic everyone thought it might be. Another three days into the wilderness unleashes another crisis, this time over the lack of water. The people grumbled against Moses, Moses went to the Lord, got the answer and fixed the problem. It is here that we read that God was testing them (Exodus 15: 25).

This would be the pattern of their journey that would last forty years: a divine test and a stubborn reaction, then another test and another bad response with more critical accusations aimed at Moses and God. Every obstacle God placed before them to cause them to look to Him with trust and confidence in His ability to answer them favorably became to them a stumbling block. God's desire was to prove to them His goodness towards them and His intentions to bless them.

> Their inability to connect the dots of God's goodness and loving kindness was further compounded by their carnal appetites. What they perceived God to be was nothing more than a powerful entity that could do amazing things - fight their battles and provide some comforts. They witnessed the demonstration of God's acts but were unwilling to know His ways. Was it beyond their capabilities to discern that this God was in fact an entity with a personality, a character and not just some impersonal force that would stand by and listen to their every whine and complaint?

They witnessed all the miraculous things that Joshua and Caleb witnessed but came away with an entirely different conclusion. Joshua and Caleb saw things with different sets of eyes and a different spirit. To them there was a personal God who came to their rescue and each event further revealed to them how committed He was to His people and how much He loved them. They saw God as an "ever present" help in time of need.

These were not indiscriminate acts of an angry God just wanting to beat up on Egyptians. These were the methodical workings of a Father who came to save His people, and not just any people but His chosen people.

One of His purposes was to reveal to them through the laws and precepts that they were in fact a chosen nation, a holy nation set apart for Gods purposes, a people that should reflect to the other nations His goodness and favor, a religion that went deeper than just lip service, sacrifice and outward acts of piety.

What became apparent was that they wanted God but only on their own terms. Through the many tests God allowed them to undergo, He was revealing to them how stubborn, rebellious and stiff- necked they really were (Deuteronomy 8:2-5).

> God could not make known His ways to the children of Israel because the children of Israel did not want to learn the ways of the Lord. The consequence of their choices was death in the wilderness. It was not a matter that they could not know His ways; they did not want to come into His ways and be taught in the matter of the issues of their hearts.
> Their natural appetites became the driving forces that led them to destruction.

God could not bring them into His Promised Land: a whole generation died in the wilderness. They were a generation of grumblers and complainers, never satisfied, always wanting more. A people chosen by God and powerfully delivered by God tragically wound up resisting God at every test and turn in the road to his or her own peril.

What kind of examples are these people to us anyway? They are an example of what we should not be or how we should not act in our relationship to God.

One of the most sobering warnings given to the church and not the children of Israel is found in Hebrews 3:7-19. This whole chapter deals with same issue of trials, testing, and knowing the ways of God. Verse 7 begins: "Therefore, just as the Holy Spirit says, today if you hear His voice, do not harden your hearts as when they provoked Me, as in the day of trial in the wilderness, Where your fathers tried Me by testing Me, and saw My works for forty years. Therefore I was angry with this generation, and said, they always go astray in their hearts; and **they did not know my ways**" (7-10, emphasis mine).

The verse states that the Holy Spirit is speaking. The same God that spoke in their wilderness is also speaking in ours. It is in the desert waste places of our walks that the Lord is testing our faithfulness. He longs to reveal to us His ways, the 'how to be' and 'how to do' like Him.

The children of Israel hardened their hearts towards God. That word harden in Greek speaks of "making something hard and dry" like a callous. How did this happen? In the day of trial or the day of temptation, this is the one incident that became the 'big one'. It is mentioned in Exodus17:7 and also in Psalms 95. We can see why, the Holy Spirit wants to bring this point home for our instruction and provide a sober warning.

Let's take a moment to review. God delivered Israel out of their bondage with ten miraculous acts. In the process He decimated Egypt's wealth, power and glory. These acts, as we stated earlier, were all witnessed by Israel and Egypt together. They walk through the Red sea as if on dry land with a wall of water on both sides. As if that was not awesome enough, God performed events that are even more miraculous. Manna, a thin crust of bread-like substance, showed up every morning except on the Sabbath for forty years and enough of it to feed three million people every time!

An Outdated Gospel

Ponder for a moment the natural logistics in providing for that many people on a daily basis. Let us average it out to a pound for each person for each day. That is a whopping three million pounds of manna per day! Over forty years, (you can do the math) that is an astronomical amount.

> There was no possible way they could have fed themselves in that desert, and there is no possible way any human effort could have provided sustenance even for one meal, let alone forty years. God was their only provision.

What about the quail? Think of it. Quail for three million hungry people! Better call in the extra caterers! In Numbers 11:31-32, we get the details as to the amount of quail God delivered by wind to their camp. The quail that dropped to the ground were two cubits thick in every direction around the camp, that's three feet thick where I come from. It goes on to say that, those who gathered least gathered ten homers full of quail.

We need to do the math here to be able to fathom the amount of meat that landed around their camp. The footnote in my Bible says that a homer is equal (in our understanding of measurement) to eleven bushels. For anyone familiar with bushels, you can put a lot of quails in one bushel. So for the sake of argument and staying on the conservative side of things, let us allow twenty quail per bushel, which in my estimate is still low when you realize a quail would be about the size of a large grapefruit. Twenty quail per bushel multiplied by eleven equals two hundred and twenty quails per person!

Now, how many people went out up pick up quail? Again this is just a guesstimate but let's say every family decided to make it a family outing, something like going to pick strawberries or apples. The scholars estimate that between two and three million people left Egypt. So let us split the difference and put that number at two and a half million. Let's be conservative and say that maybe two million people would go out and gather quail. We need to remember there were no sick, lame or lazy folks that were going to get their meat picked for them.

So, we have two million people and the ones who picked the least picked eleven bushels, what did the others pick? Here is the equation: 2,000,000 people x 220 quail (20 quails per bushel x 11 bushels) = 440,000,000 birds daily!

And if each quail weighed approximately one pound feathers and all; that would come up to a whopping four hundred and forty million pounds or twenty two thousand tons! That is a whole lot of feather plucking.

We cannot forget the water logistics while we are at it. The 'rock' that followed them in the wilderness provided a whole lot of water. We tend to think of provision for the people, but let us not forget all the livestock in our equation. Walking around in a hot dry desert, plus washing clothes, personal hygiene and a whole lot of healthy livestock, required an exorbitant amount of water every day. The livestock also ate manna, what else was there? There were no bales of hay falling from the sky! The point being, how could anyone of a sound mind witness all the miraculous events on a daily basis for forty years and remain hard hearted and unbelieving?

The day they tested the Lord was a day of provocation – *parapikrasmos*. This Greek word is made up of two words, *para*, which means 'alongside' and *pickraino*, which means 'to make bitter'. That day was marked as a day that bitterness came alongside or we could say became a part of or so closely attached itself to it. You could not separate the two; it was a day that left God with a bitter taste in His mouth.

> I hope we all understand that God doesn't walk around with bitterness in His heart towards them or anyone else for that matter, but certain events like this one - and we may have experienced them ourselves - tend to be remembered in a negative way and leave a bad taste in one's mouth.

An Outdated Gospel

This event, as I stated earlier, is recorded in Exodus 17:7. Let's remember all the logistical points we've just read and how God just continued to answer their request despite their constant grumbling and murmuring.

Here's the verse: "And he [Moses] named that place Massah [test] and Meribah [quarrel] because of the quarrel of the sons of Israel, and because they tested the Lord, saying, is the Lord among us or not?" Hello, is anybody home? Of course, it seems ridiculously simple to us. Of course, He has to be with you!

In Hebrews 3:10 which is quoted from Psalms 95:10 we read, "… they do always err in their hearts.…" It always comes down to a heart issue, always, always and always. That word "err" is the Greek word *planao* and it means "to roam in regards to safety, truth or virtue; to go astray, deceive, seduce" (Vines Expository of Biblical Words).

Somehow the signs and wonders did not penetrate their heart. We might think that seeing everything they saw would make one more pliable in God's hands and softer towards Him but not so as we read these passages.

Their ability to process all the wonders around them seemed to always add up to a wrong tally and a wrong conclusion. God said they erred in their hearts; their hearts roamed away from the truth, virtue and ultimately from the safety parameters of God's protection into judgment. What was supposed to draw them into a closer relationship turned them away. All their needs were met; what more did they need?

Deep down inside, they did not want to know His ways; they only wanted a higher power that would provide their wants and cravings for them on demand. They did not want the transforming hand of a personal God messing with their insides; they preferred to give Him lip service, outward acts of sacrifice and homage. They wanted to remain their own person. How deceived they were, not realizing that this God was indeed very different then all the other gods in Egypt and even the ones they carried around with them in the wilderness for the next forty years.

I cannot get away from the fact of how similar we all can be to the children of Israel even though the truth of their error is so obvious. I guess it is of no surprise why they are an example to us. We have all seen the faithful, miraculous hand of God in our lives in countless ways. It may not be manna or the parting of the Red Sea, but salvation, deliverance, healing, jobs, finances: these are no less the signs and the wonders of a loving God working in our midst on a regular basis. Do not be surprised that while we are moving on in the things of God and as we pursue Him and experience the good and awesome acts of God that a 'desert place' is being prepared for us.

How is it that we miss this stark point: we are not in control of our own circumstances!

> Our wilderness is meant to undo us, to strip us of all the layers of religion and selfishness, to bring us to the end of our own reasoning, strength and natural abilities - an end of ourselves. In this wilderness place, we cry out to Him because we cannot provide for ourselves. It's impossible; think of the logistics.

We do not know where we are going or how to get out of it, so how do we know what we need in the midst of our trials. To remain alive and healthy, to stay on track and not get deceived or seduced in the process, is beyond us. We Christians cannot, I repeat cannot get through this journey on our own intellect or resourcefulness.

The danger for us, like the Israelites, is to tally up all the information and come to a wrong conclusion as they did. Why? Because they wanted to live for the moment, they were not in the least interested in God's ways.

The trials exposed every hidden attitude and mindset they carried tucked away deep down inside. They were amazed at the wonders and enjoyed the buffet but had a dim view of being educated into the higher principles of the Spirit of the Almighty.

We would rather God not mess with our insides or our plans: 'please God, keep your hands off of my personal things, but I'm open to your creature comforts and blessings.' So when the difficult times come, and they will come for everyone who names the name of Jesus Christ, how will we process our wilderness journey? Will our hearts become hard because we are not liking our trek in the desert and so we put God to the test and charge Him with not caring or being off somewhere else and letting us fend for ourselves? Will we test Him by demanding He provide for us certain things when He has already deemed those things as unnecessary and harmful, but we continue to insist that He provide it now and just the way we want it.

We must be careful what we ask for since we just might get it and regret it and it just might distract us from the holy and narrow track that God is laying out for us as we walk humbly and softly before Him. How similar we really are to the Israelites, and it is no wonder; we are of the same human nature that we must choose to crucify.

There is a rest for the child of God in the midst of the desert. It is not in the absence of adversity or hardship that we find this place. Our promised land - the place of our coming into abundance in God's promises - is to be sure a place of fulfillment and purpose.

> Nevertheless, our promised land, as good and fruitful as it can be, will never yield the rich fruit of 'Eschol'. Here in the midst of giants and walled cities two men pressed in to their assigned territory and returned with fruit so large that they carried one cluster of grapes on a pole between the two of them. The wilderness yields a harvest unlike and I believe superior to the routine life of Canaan.

Learning the ways of God will pay superior dividends. For the believer he or she may find himself or herself as Moses being placed in the cleft of the Rock right beside the Lord Himself, a brief moment of unparalleled glory as we behold the Lord passing by.

We need to get God's perspective on why He does things a certain way. We may see hardship, disappointment and even sorrow over our present circumstances, but the transformed mindset of the over comer is to accept the present condition, quit complaining about all the hardships and search this land of our wandering because God has great reward in it for us since He led us here.

It is our land, our proving grounds, our place to excel. When the Israelites entered the Promised Land the manna ceased once they ate of the produce of that land. Their ways of life were returning in some measure back to normal - the ability to provide for themselves from the land. Although God was still working His wonders around them by displacing the inhabitants of the land, a new season was upon them: the wilderness was behind them and a new frontier before them.

Let us lean into Him in the trials of our lives when things no longer make sense or seem fair or right; it's at this juncture that the Joshua's and the Caleb's emerge and it will be said of us, these are men and woman of another spirit.

> Our rest is in Him, not a destination or a prophetic word fulfilled as good and wonderful as that may be. Our rest is a heart attitude, a place of repose, an abiding trust in the center of turmoil and strife, good times or bad, the deep satisfaction of knowing that He is always there; we are in His constant embrace, without lack, without fear. This is Psalms 23 walked out in the reality zones of our lives.

Chapter 9

Testing 101

There are times when the line between being tested and being tempted is somewhat blurred. Much of our inability to discern between the two might be because we are up to our ears in the circumstances and the emotional energy being produced is wreaking havoc in our hearts and minds.

In the previous chapter, we looked at the children of Israel in their wilderness journey with all its challenges. From our perspective, we have the benefit of hindsight, not being personally involved and having God's final word on their matter (Read Psalms 78).

The main purpose of God's testing was to reveal to them what was in their hearts. This was not for God's benefit or information but for the children of Israel: God already knew what was there.

So the million dollar question that should be asked here is: why do I need to know what is in my heart if God already knows? This brings us to the million dollar answer: because I need to see the true condition of my heart when I am confronted with a choice for or against, follow or stay, embrace or reject.

When God reveals to us the condition of our hearts through the trials and the adversity we encounter, everything in us is put into gear and our thought processes begin analyzing and interpreting all the data.

What has been taught to us in the form of our formal education at school, the instruction at home, on the job training, what we have picked up along the way on our own or imparted to us by others - everything is being filtered through what we have come to know by theory or practical experience and our responses and reactions will be a direct result of this data.

> Take in to consideration all our moral guidance, any religious upbringing or the lack thereof, the philosophies of this one or that one where we just picked through them all like a smorgasbord. We embraced our favorites and to top it all off, add our family genetics and dispositions, dysfunctions - what a mix! It's through those filters we observe the world around us, for better or worse. The truth is "we don't see things as they are, we see things as we are" (Anais Nin).

I do not know about you but there are a great many things that just rub me the wrong way; here is one. You are in a long line of traffic and you're just creeping along. There is only one lane at this point, the other lane is blocked off up ahead and so we all form a single line and wait our turn to get through the bottleneck intent on emerging with a good attitude on the other side. Everything is ok until these other drivers start passing you in the other lane, you know the one that is blocked off up ahead. Oh no! These people won't abide by our code of conduct; they have the audacity to not only pass us - we who are waiting patiently just creeping along - but they then try to squeeze in ahead of us who have been patient in line. No way am I going to allow them to cut in!

> We all have our own pet peeves right - the product or the not so good fruit of a great many variables in our makeup, and all of which will come under the watchful eye of our Father. These variables, attitudes or just plain dysfunctional behaviours are what we so often want to dismiss as nothing – 'that's just me or that's how I do things'. We want to excuse our behaviour and attitudes while being critical of others who demonstrate the same lousy conduct. The sad truth is we can go on for years stepping on other people's feelings, blowing them away with our quick wit and sharp tongues oblivious to the collateral damage being heaved on all those around us.

The appeal of others cannot penetrate the hard shell of our pride and self- righteousness. We are not ready to hear their corrective criticism at least that is how we view it to be. So when David writes in Psalms 139:14 that we are fearfully and wonderfully made, I do not think he was talking about this issue.

Some of us are more pliable and only a little persuasion will be enough for us to get the point, repent and make the course correction that is needed to restore peace, regain vision and resume our journey. Others are harder nuts to crack, while even others come to a place where they refuse to crack, scary!

For most of us this fact may be obvious: we are not large holding tanks that retain every little lesson we have ever learned. The instruction we get today in a particular area may be the same instruction we will need in six months, yet we tend to forget the lessons, and many times the circumstances and landscape of this trial are different and we have a hard time figuring out the answer.

To do well in the kingdom we need to remain humble and teachable. 'Lord what is the answer to the test I am in?' We are allowed to ask Him. In fact, we can ask those around us, 'what's the answer to the test I am in right now?' It is an open book test anyway; we can open our Bibles and search for the answer. God **does** want us to pass the test. He does not want us to flunk, no matter what we may feel in the midst of our test. My willingness to confess my need and my inability to know the next step allows God to be gracious in his application of practical on the job training and grace.

This cross, this test, is the custom-made product that will be a catalyst in me to stir the very areas of my heart that God is interested in dealing with at a given point in time.

> We would all do well to take careful heed to what God is putting His finger on. Anytime issues keep passing across the bow of our spiritual ships, we had better pay attention; the chances are we will not make any more progress until each issue is confronted and we are able to deal honestly with them before God.

The snakes, the bitter waters and all the other lacks were divinely appointed for the children of Israel; there were no coincidences or accidents in their wilderness. It's tragic that even after so many years the lesson were still rejected; what was meant to produce life by passing the test, produced death. They rejected not only the lesson but also the teacher.

We may as well start embracing the path of Gods choosing for us, as easy or hard as that may be. He wrote the script over our lives; we may struggle with that but it is nonetheless true. We are His; we are not our own. The alternative is to go back to our former taskmaster - not a great option.

My life can only find its true fulfillment and purpose as it is surrendered to Him on a continual basis. It is not a onetime deal.

The other obvious truth that we dare not acknowledge at times is that as a blood bought born again Christian everything that comes into our lives has been filtered through His hands. That can be a hard one to wrap your head around. You mean everything? Yes everything. How big is our God anyway? Let us lay out this premise.

We begin with the fact that God has known us for a long, long time. 2 Timothy 1:9 sheds light on this matter: "who [God] has saved us and called us with a holy calling not according to our works, but according to His purpose and grace which was granted us in Christ Jesus from all eternity." We have been in the purposes of God for a long time, all of eternity. What we do and how we respond is of our own choosing.

Another verse (and there are many) is found in Psalms 139:16b: "The days that were ordained for me, when as yet there was not one of them." God's interest in us and the purposes for our lives pre-date our own plans and aspirations. This mighty God has had us in His heart and His eternal purpose for us is more than just chance or a dice throw. I think we all have trouble trying to figure out how in the world can God know us along with the other six billion plus people on the planet and know us most intimately in every little detail and even to know our thoughts from afar. Wow!

Our peculiar ways and quirks, all the pluses and minuses of our thinking, the hairs on our head today and the loss of the ones we will mourn over tomorrow: how big can He be? We have no idea but with the universe around us and the million and one marvelous spectacles of life at our doorstep, the evidence points to someone without boundaries or limitations awesome beyond words.

What if we were to put together a team of specialist whose only purpose was to take care of our needs and to plan our futures, meet our emotional and psychological needs, guide and instruct us in every facet of life, study our behaviour in good times and in bad? Would this team ever be able to know us and be acquainted with the true person we really are? Would their input and analysis impart into our spirit man the character we all desire to have apart from the work of God? I think not, only because we really do not know who we are ourselves.

We are all on the road of self-discovery. Every trial, each relationship, every phase and season of our lives surfaces new emotions and feelings. We are often surprised about our reaction to information. The things we say and do may at times embarrass us or come back to haunt us. How will we react or adjust our thinking to our new surroundings, will we reject the new, will we adapt our lifestyles to the changes or harden ourselves because of the pain and adversity we have experienced?

We are complex beings; no one can know our thoughts and our choices beforehand, not even us. Job's life and trials make a captivating and provoking story. You cannot help but feel great compassion and sorrow for Job. The magnitude of his pain and suffering causes one to shudder. I think I speak for most when I say there is no way I could see myself coming through that kind of pain with my integrity still intact and my faith purified as gold as his was. As I make this statement I realize that this is most likely prompted by fear - paralyzing fear that acts like an invisible hand around one's neck trying to choke the life out of you.

I remember the stories of the many different missionaries I have read about who left every known comfort of their day to carve out an existence in another country or culture. Untold scores of these Godly saints buried their spouses and children in the soils of foreign lands. They themselves were subject to thirst, starvation, disease and the constant threat of death from their enemies.

> What in heaven's name motivates a person to give up so much willingly? For them their love for God far outweighed the pangs of fear tearing at their insides. They were not super men or women in the sense that they were superior in all manner of godly attributes; rather if they were superior, it was in their intent on being obedient to the call of God. It was not about weighing the pros and cons of their decision and its consequences. It came down to the narrow road of choice, not a choice that will benefit me but a choice that benefits God's kingdom; the meeting of two wills produces a cross and they chose to carry theirs.

Here is a brief example of sacrifice we seldom see or hear about; it is an extravagant picture of love and passion that marked an era in church history which opened the dark continents to the light of Christ.

A great soldier of the cross, William Hotchkiss, told the story of his early life in Kenya, East Africa. Missionaries in the late 1800s had to live solely on native food, for they took along very little equipment and no special food. Once he lived for two and a half months on beans, sour milk and even at times on ants. Another time for weeks on end, he went without the commonest of all necessities, salt. He mentioned his fear of attacks from man-eating lions.

After long accounts of their sufferings and the cost of many lives, he concludes by saying "but don't talk to me about sacrifice. It is no sacrifice. In the face of the superlative joy of that one overwhelming experience, the joy of flashing that miracle word, Savior, for the first time to a great tribe that had never heard it before, I can never think of these past forty years in terms of sacrifice. I saw Christ and His cross and I did this because I love Him."

Then he quoted Watt's matchless song:
"When I survey the wondrous Cross
On which the Prince of Glory died
My richest gain I count but loss, and pour contempt on all my pride
Were the whole realm of nature mine
That were a present far too small.
Love so amazing, so divine,
Demands my soul, my life, my all."

> Another missionary was asked: do you like your work? "Like this work?" he replied, "no, my wife and I do not like dirt. We have reasonably refined sensibilities. We don't like crawling into vile huts through goat refuse. We don't like association with ignorant, filthy, brutish people. But is a man to do nothing for Christ which he does not like? God pity such a one. Liking or disliking has nothing to do with it. We have orders to go and we go. Love constrains us."

We do not often think of responding to a work or ministry as a test. Yet it is exactly that in a nutshell. The end result of any test is our ability to not only know the subject matter but in a more practical way our ability to apply it. It usually requires a process although it does not always have to. Since the children of Israel are still somewhat fresh in our minds lets us visit that story again, briefly.

God tells Moses to go down to Egypt and tell Pharaoh to let His people go. Moses obeyed God's instruction and did only what he was told. Pharaoh lets the people go free after some convincing wonders and they are off to the desert. Moses is passing his call and instruction with aces. Everyone is following Divine instructions as they head into the wilderness. Now the complications start. God orchestrates the conditions so that things are not so easy and convenient. The people start to manifest a very dark side, which escalates into rebellion and accusations. They become obstinate and stiff-necked. Therefore, what could have been a straight walk across the desert turns into a forty year hike with a whole lot of death and suffering. Lesson learned? No.

Response is the key, and it certainly has to be the right one; not any response will do as we see here with them. Moses gets it; Joshua and Caleb get it. We are not in charge and we don't call the shots. We really cannot change a whole lot on our own, but in obedience we become yoked to the Almighty and we pass the test.

The distance between our unwillingness to be conformed and the end result of embracing the cross is what we could term as another lap around the mountain.

Jonah's unwillingness to obey God by delivering the message to the Ninevites resulted in a whole lot of unnecessary hardship not in the original script. God's desire and purpose for Jonah was about being obedient and heading in the direction of Nineveh. Jonah's choice for all of his own personal reasons propelled him in the opposite direction.

Because of God's great love and superior purposes this ordeal was far from over. God was going to have his man, and in the process teach Jonah a thing or two about His great love and compassion for these people. In this process He provided a few object lessons to try and get through to Jonah's anger issue which was directed at God (thank God He is so patient with us)

Jonah, like the rest of us, had figured God out to some degree by drawing the conclusion that God would relent, have mercy and not bring the judgment that Jonah was being sent to proclaim. So Jonah figured, 'why go, I'm the one who's going to look bad, and God - well I know he's going to forgive them after they repent, so why go at all?'

The measure and scope of our test is always in our simple obedience. Tied to obedience is the training, the equipping and the anointing and God provides the results.

The interesting thing to remember here is what God considers important as He asks, directs and at times commands us to serve Him. He is mindful of who we are and all our little shortcomings that are about to be stretched in a way they have never been stretched before - this is going to hurt!

With the 'yes' response, our will is already in gear as we move towards God's desired ends. The 'making or the conforming' to make us willing does not come in to play right at the start. We may need some persuasion a little later as we understand the bigger picture of what He may be asking, but for now we are on the yes side of things.

> So many of the Old Testament characters had their private discussions with God, and this is very normal. We do not always see things God's way or understand His methods or ways - nor will we ever fully understand (Isaiah 55:9-11). What really happens in this discussion phase is that we get a chance to vent our frustrations, fears and our inabilities to do what He has called us to do, and yes, at times, even our unwillingness to do what He is calling us to do!

You know, no time, no money, no ideas - we just cannot figure it out; why would God ask me? Then we have another great idea:

why don't You ask someone else? They have everything it takes to do exactly this kind of thing that You're asking me to do. All the while, we rehearse our story in His ears over a period of time and we find out after all our drama we have not changed God's mind in the slightest.

> What follows could be called a meltdown or our internal crisis. We have exhausted all our mental, emotional and rational arguments but to no avail. At this point most of us are in a broken and humbled place. We have heard the Lord and sense that He is asking of us certain things. We place before Him our best arguments and come away realizing that God will not be dissuaded. Now after the tears and the pleas, we then choose to obey, and we do so because we know deep down God has our best interest in mind at every bend and turn in the road of our lives. He has also backed us up into a corner for a purpose. He is aware that we feel overwhelmed and inadequate at times and at other times we figure God would be better off if He would just adjust His plans a little, be more reasonable and see things our way. A little give and take right Lord?

The danger always exists - and believe me it's factored into God's equation - that the devil will come along and muddy up the waters. The enemy understands our human nature better than we do. Remember the devil is only allowed to come in for a time and within certain parameters to tempt us. This is not to say that we in our own self-will and rebellion cannot open the door to his schemes and strategies beyond the scope of God's purposes for us. What he is looking for is any ground we may give him to move us from the place of God's rest into confusion, doubt and turmoil as he tries to whip up all our natural impulses and get us to concentrate on our own personal self-interest.

For instance, if we had been seeking God for a particular thing in our lives and after a season of prayer we sense that He is saying no, the easy route to take is to embrace the answer, accept no as the perfect will for my life for now and for this situation and move on: God has something better.

Depending on how important this thing may be to us and how much stock we have in it, a 'yes and amen response' may not be too heartfelt. Now we may start getting upset wondering why God would not allow this good thing to happen for us. (This thing mentioned here could not be something clearly taught in scripture as sinful or could lead to sin).

Now our adversary will try to bring in the character of God into question on most issues of our lives. It started in the Garden and continues to this day. 'Did God really say? God does not want you to enjoy things; He is holding back from you; He will bless others but not you.' Too many sins, not spiritual enough and on and on the barrage of thoughts continues.

Even in this entire ordeal, God has allowed the enemy to be the instrument of doubt or accusation to sound out the depth of our hearts and reveal them to us. This is in order that we will deal honestly and humbly with the stuff that floats to the surface. This is not a time to sidestep the issues at hand. He has gone to great lengths to fish this area up out of the hidden recesses and desires to deal with them head on for our sake. Yet to deny or sidestep the obvious condition at hand would be to push us into deception and further darkness in a particular area. It is not time to play the 'blame game' either.

It is at this juncture that we need to take our stand, choose to submit to God's will and purposes trusting in His goodness and then resist the devil's onslaught as we are tucked away within the hedge of God's protection. Job's life is a prime example of what is taking place in the spiritual background of our lives.

If we fail to see God as over 'all' then we will see Him with limitations.

> We are the children of our Heavenly Father; His gaze does not overlook one item no matter how small or minute as it relates to our upbringing; nothing is left to chance.
>
> He is the initiator in the trials and testing of our lives. He sets the boundaries, the periods and the intensity of our valley experiences, like it or not.

There is no devil free to assault us at his will. For the blood bought saint of God, his or her abiding place is in the Most High and if that be the case, which demon has the power to assail us in the arms of Christ without permission?

I will refer back to the story of Job to highlight a conversation God was having with Satan, we pick it up in chapter 1:8-12:

> "And the Lord said to Satan, "Have you considered My servant Job? For there is no one like him on the earth, a blameless and upright man, fearing God and turning away from evil."
>
> "Then Satan answered the Lord, Does Job fear God for nothing? Hast Thou not made a hedge about him and his house and all that he has on every side? Thou hast blessed the work of his hands, and his possessions have increased in the land. But put forth Thy hand now and touch all that he has: he will surely curse Thee to Thy face."
>
> Then the Lord said to Satan, "behold all that he has is in your power, only do not put forth your hand on him." So Satan departed from the presence of the Lord."

You will notice in verse eight that it is God initiating the test; in fact, He is bragging on Job and his good character. Satan's reply reveals that there is a protective "hedge" around the saint of God and even Satan is not able to penetrate it unless God gives him the authority to do it. That should be a great relief to all of us. Our backs are covered saints, unless, as I have mentioned earlier, we choose to walk out from under the protective wings of the Almighty (Psalm 91:1-4) (Proverbs 26:27).

God also places certain restrictions on Satan and the degree that he may assault Job. In this case, his children and all his possessions fall into the parameters of Satan's power. Then in another conversation, God allows Satan to afflict Job's body with boils.

We have to read stories like this from the security of God's promises to us as His beloved children; otherwise fear tends to settle in and cause us to see our good Father as someone who indiscriminately sends disease and plaques on people and makes their lives miserable and unbearable. Actually this is the picture that the world paints of God (Christians as well), and they say 'if there is a God and He afflicts innocent little children with cancer then I can't believe in such a God'. The good news is He is not such a God.

Even our ideas of the Old Testament's nasty, angry God are inaccurate if we believe Him to be the giver of sickness and diseases. He is the same yesterday today and forever (Hebrews 13:8). He is neither schizophrenic nor double minded; a careful study reveals a God who was patient, longsuffering and merciful to the nations that walked away from Him and spurned His laws and precepts and in His face chose to serve other gods after having known the truth. Then in His measured judgment punished those nations after having appealed to them to repent and turn from their sins.

> It is odd that sometimes we think that, as human beings, we are more graceful and merciful than God is towards others (at least until the next time when we are cut off in traffic).

God sent prophets repeatedly to pagan nations whose ancestors had known the true God to warn them of judgment if they did not turn away from their ungodly practices. Some of these practices were as wicked as it gets. They sacrificed their own children on an altar that opened up into a furnace and burned their children alive - that's one example. God's appeal to them was not from a frustrated ornery character that was just waiting to whack somebody on the head if they got out of line.

As He is a Father to us, is He not also a Father to them as well: full of love and compassion, even as they pursued their own lusts and erroneous ways? The love He had for all His people was exemplified in the heart and cries of those same men who went to those nations and cried out to them as Noah did in his generation for a hundred years as he built the ark. Even in the face of all those appeals, they laughed and scoffed at God's goodness and mercy and refused the safety of the Ark, a symbol of God's unmovable, unshakeable abiding presence in the shadow of the imminent judgment.

I realize that what I am saying is in defense of God's good character, and it is. The reason I am going to some length here is to expose our somewhat distorted view of God.

We say the New Testament God is different from the Old Testament God. That cannot be the case, as I previously mentioned. He is the same (Hebrews 13:8). God has always looked for men and woman who would look to Him with faith and trust and would desire Him and His ways. Nothing has changed in this regard.

A favorite Old Testament scripture that captures this idea is found in 2 Chronicles16:9: "For the eyes of the Lord move to and fro throughout the whole earth that He may strongly support those whose heart is completely His."

Through the pain and tears of tribulation, our night season of the soul is tailored by God to not only fit the vessels unique ability to endure the adversity but also to raise us up into an abiding, keeping grace - a new dimension of His Presence in our lives. It's not in vain, dear saint of God that we are led into the fiery trials.

Much of what I have said is very basic. Yet even in regards to the subject of going through tests and the fiery trials this teaching of the Cross is slowly fading into the sunset on the Western Christian horizon.

> To go through our Christian walk and not understand the ways and purposes of God in the midst of our trials is unthinkable and tragic. To go through adversity and wrongly conclude it is all about the devil, or some kind of Karma is to miss the purpose of God's discipline and instruction.

It is imperative that we catch this one truth, if nothing else. Yes, the sufferings of Job were terrible; none of us in our right mind would willingly choose to volunteer for such trials. However, what is so often missed or just willfully dismissed from our radar screen is that God chose Job. I'll say it again - God chose Job and initiated the test.

Finally, I thought Job's words to be most appropriate. In light of everything he went through, it amazes me every time I read his testimony of faith in the very storm of his life:

"But He knows the way I take;
When He has tried me, I shall come forth as gold.
My foot has held fast to His path;
I have kept His way and not turned aside.
I have not departed from the command of His lips;
I have treasured the words of His mouth more than my necessary food."
(Job 23:10-12)

Job's ability to remain not only standing, but also victorious is found in the fact that God's word remained the source of his sustenance. His declaration was not some rehearsed script he had learned as a child, pulled conveniently from his memory bank, mere words without life or conviction.

These words were galvanized to his heart in the furnace of his affliction with all the faith and confidence from Almighty God Himself. He was not being arrogant or cocky as he declared that he would stay grounded on the path of God's choosing despite the tragedies on every side. He understood that the word of God was to him as an eternal Rock on which to stand and he refused all other contradictory counsel, even from his own wife.

"Behold how happy is the man whom God reproves'
So do not despise the discipline of the Almighty" (Job 5: 17).

Chapter 10

Temptation 101

After repeatedly looking at the life of Job over the course of many years, I have come away with a better understanding of how God directs the events and circumstances around my own life. One cannot get away from the fact that His fingerprints are all over our trials, adversity and wilderness experiences.

Any serious inspection of Job's life would rightly conclude that God alone is 'guilty' of testing His servant and allowing him to suffer hardship. Joe Citizen who lives in the world at large would read this same story of Job and conclude that the God of the Bible, if He does exist, is nothing but a big, mean bully and therefore is not a God that he could love and serve. This is another miscalculation of epic proportions.

The man of the world and far too many Christians see only through the prism of their ideal picture of God. He is the God of their own creation, not the One we read about in scripture.

There is a great underlying question here that we must all answer for our own satisfaction not to mention for our own core belief: is God good or isn't He? Some would venture to say 'of course God is good, He blesses me and provides all my needs; in fact He would never do anything to hurt me.'

Depending on one's interpretation of 'hurt me'; many see the testing's of God as not coming from God, but from the devil.

They would view any kind of adversity as being totally negative, inconvenient, stressful and from the devil himself. The God of their own making is more of the Santa Claus type: a grandfather sort of character, full of good cheer, passing out gift to all, not wanting to hurt anyone's feelings and treating everyone fairly. The non-intrusive God is one that understands when we've had a bad day and will leave us alone if we decide to drift over into some 'harmless gratifications' to unwind and release the day's tension. We do not want a God or any preacher for that matter to be beating up on us about sin and holy living after a long week of slugging it out at work, raising kids and just plain living in this rat race.

> The truth is God is good and because He is good, He has laid out for us a life with many obstacles. In his goodness He has prearranged misunderstandings, agony, suffering and rejection. Every one of these things in one form or another are awaiting us on the same road we are travelling on right now, and the best part is - it has our name on it. Nothing is left to chance for the child of God.

The Potter who is forming the clay has a great interest in the small details.

The landscape may have changed, but the lesson remains the same. The Lord Himself will guide our journey. He is committed to us even when we blow it. The boot camp of God's discipline is a lifetime of instruction, correction, and yes, a great deal of grace and encouragement that will transform me into that godly person I keep crying out to be.

Let us settle the matter. "Furthermore, we had earthly fathers to discipline us, and we respected them; shall we not much more be subject to the Father of spirits and live? For they disciplined us for a short time as seemed best to them, but He disciplines us for our good, that we may share His holiness" (Hebrews 12:9:10).

An Outdated Gospel

I would like you to take a look at the words "test" and "tempt" and their meanings from the dictionary. The first is the word we have already spent a great deal of time with in the previous chapter:

> TEST: (noun) a means of assessing the quality, capabilities, reliability or endurance of somebody or something; a trial. A series of questions or exercises for measuring the knowledge intelligence, ability, ect. of an individual or group. A real life situation that reveals the worth or quality of something or somebody by SUBJECTING them to stress, difficulties, etc.
>
> TEMPT: (verb) to make (somebody) feel strongly inclined to do something: to attract or appeal to (somebody) to try to persuade (somebody) to do something wicked immoral or unwise by the promise of PLEASURE or GAIN

Notice the distinct difference in the meaning of these two words. The word "test" describes a process to ascertain worth, quality, knowledge, understanding or ability from a person or thing.

In our formal education, we were tested on a regular basis to reveal the depth and scope of our understanding in a particular subject. The teacher did not sit around and try to figure out ways to trick us or confuse us and thereby fail us. The teacher tests the class to discover whether the class has grasped the lessons taught, and from the answers of his or her students, the teacher will also be able to fine tune the lesson or alter the method of teaching.

> The whole idea of testing is to determine what we know and what we still have not been able to grasp. The next step the teacher would take would be to identify all the errors on the test and bring them up again at the next class for another review. It is not about trying to fail us or make us feel stupid. It is all about learning the material so that we can move on to the next grade level.

Instruction, testing, instruction, testing, more instruction more testing...

Now the word "tempt" is associated with evil or wrongdoing. The definition paints a picture of someone trying to persuade you to do or say something that up to this point you have refrained from, with the promise of pleasure or gain attached to it. This pleasure or gain is the irresistible honey set out to attract the circling flies. In order to tempt successfully the trap must be baited with the intended victim's appetites in mind - not just any bait will do.

This dictionary meaning ties in perfectly with a verse found in James and it also makes the distinction between tests and tempt and which does what. "Let no one say when he is tempted, I am being tempted by God; for God cannot be tempted by evil, and He Himself does not tempt anyone. But each one is tempted when he is carried away and enticed by his own lust" (James 1:13-14).

"Let no one say" [that's you and I] "when he is tempted" [we are all tempted and on a regular basis] "I am being tempted by God," [an impossibility so we should not say it] "for God cannot be tempted by evil," [an obvious Biblical truth] "and He Himself does not tempt anyone" another obvious Biblical truth. "BUT, each one is tempted WHEN he is drawn away [carried away] and enticed by his own lust". (Emphasis mine)

The two words "drawn away" is the Greek word *ex el' ko'* and it means "to drag forth, to entice, to draw away by lust". It is used metaphorically here as in hunting or fishing to describe how the game is lured away from its haunt; so man's lust allures him from the safety of his self restraint.

James is shooting straight from the hip here. In plain English he is saying, 'Let us quit blaming God when we are tempted; He's unable to be tempted and He does not use evil, wicked or injurious methods to lure us away from the safety of our own self restraint.'

> Our own lust is used as a lure to entice us just like a fish biting on the shiny new lure that was dragged in front of its nose and it just could not let it go by without swallowing it. On the same note, the devil has gotten a whole lot of blame for things that we ourselves were guilty of. The devil did not make us do it. We did it!

Someone once said that temptation is in itself neutral: it is neither good nor bad. It is what a person chooses in the midst of it. I am not sure I would agree with that premise.

If God Himself will not use methods that result in injury or wickedness am I to conclude that something or someone that will allure me to do evil is neutral. I do not think so.

An example of this would be a former alcoholic. He has not had a drink for a whole year. He is doing everything he knows to stay on the wagon - avoiding bars altogether and any function with any hint where alcohol might be present. He is aware of his problem and is working hard to stay sober.

Now how would we look at a friend or an acquaintance that invites him over to watch a football game with the guys and during the game breaks out the booze and passes it around all the while knowing of his friend's struggle. I would not call that man a friend any longer.

He is either "one fry short of a happy meal" or he does not really love his friend. His purpose and intent could only be to feel good about himself and his own appetite for booze and thereby put a temptation or an obstacle in another man's way. Misery loves company, so why not try to re-enslave the person and gain another drinking buddy.

So would this temptation be considered neutral? I think not. This is a temptation meant to strongly persuade someone to do something he himself had mustered up the self-restraint to resist and avoid. This scenario was not enacted by God or orchestrated by our loving Father. Love was not the motivating factor here. It was a set up to cause this man to stumble. It was not about testing him or assessing his qualities or worth; it was meant to lure him away from his resolve and self-restraint and hook him afresh with the lure of a former bondage. The so-called friend, out of his own bondage and selfishness, was being used as a tool to re-awaken this mans former addiction and once again try to plunge him back into his former oppression.

Where is God in this picture? I do not think God was on a vacation; He was very aware of what was transpiring. Since our world is a fallen world and we are all fallen people there is a whole lot of stuff going down that God is not part of. Because evil things happen to good, godly people, it does not mean they received it by the direct hand and will of God.

> God does not interject Himself into every situation that befalls us. He does not appear in our every 'dark night of the soul' to deliver us out of them, even when evil strategies have conspired to destroy our faith and testimony.

In Psalms 34:19 we read, "many are the afflictions of the righteous; but the Lord delivers him out of them all." We quote certain scriptures and we see them as blanket promises of protection that safeguard us from the calamities of everyday life. The scriptures we rehearse and commit to our memory are the words of God. These promises are not meant to shield us form every mishap, disappointment, harm or failure as much as they are meant to sustain the man or woman of God in the center of all the turmoil. It is up to God's discretion to deliver us, not my ability to quote scripture. The promises I believe are meant to carry me through but not necessarily take me out.

For whatever reason, God's purposes will take precedence over our prayer and faith for deliverance in our afflictions. We fail to realize at times that God in His sovereign providence chooses to arrange our circumstances and steers us right into the heart of the problem much to our dismay. There is more to the picture than what we can see from our vantage point.

Even with Biblical promises, God may decide, as in the case of Joseph, not to deliver him in the season Joseph would have wanted. In fact, Joseph would have chosen to bypass the accusation by Potiphar's wife and the thirteen years he spent in prison.

We often times carry the false notion that God's prime purpose for us is to keep us happy and comfortable, when in fact God is actively keeping His promise to us.

The story of Joseph is not unique. We would have done things differently and Joseph may have never become the Prime minister under Pharaoh and thus Joseph's family would have perished in the famine quite possibly squelching the nation of Israel in its infancy.

"The natural man does not accept the things of the Spirit of God; for they are foolishness to him and he cannot understand them because they are spiritually appraised" (1 Corinthians 2:14). As Christians, we mistakenly mold God to our limited range of thinking and possibilities which causes us a whole lot of grief because He does not remain in our box and we are left bewildered. We believe we have the best plan for our own spiritual well-being and we line up all the verses of scripture to confirm exactly how our lives are going to play out. And the choices we make in the midst of our afflictions have a direct effect on the outcome.

Then God allows a 'Joseph déjà vu' to happen to us. An incident at work happens and we are wrongly accused of something that is entirely bad. Right out of nowhere and bang our lives are thrust into chaos, confusion and a whole lot of pain. What happened? God could have prevented all of this, but He chose not to as in the case of Joseph.

Life is about to change drastically and it is no fault of our own. However, since we are the favoured children of God, what appears to be the end of our world is really pressing us into a new and certainly different dimension that God has ordained. So we cry out, why, why did this of all things have to happen?

> Answer: because this incident, this seeming tragedy from our perspective is the 'vehicle' God designed to take us to another level. Suddenly the handle on our lives has dropped to the floor. Nothing makes sense at this stage and we have nothing to offer God by way of advice or declarations. We are barely hanging on at times to our own faith and sanity. Has anyone been asked by God lately to offer up their Isaac on the altar?

"Curse God and die," said Job's wife. Trust me, this is not advice that any of us need to hear in our fiery furnace. It is here that we are most vulnerable.

The instrument that afflicts us and shoots the fiery arrows our way is motivated by a malignant bent for our demise; he has no other desire for us than to see us rise up and curse God because of the severity of our trials.

The devil would like nothing more than to devour our trust in God with his mental assaults. They are designed to bring confusion and to stir up any and every carnal appetite to its insatiable zenith and then beat us down with so much guilt and condemnation that we can no longer feel God's presence or hear His tender voice of mercy and grace. In turn, we harden our hearts and continue our downward spiral. Sometimes it is difficult to put this all in perspective when you are in the middle of it.

Again, in the story of Job Satan is conversing with God. We read that it is God's idea to initiate the test of Job's character. It almost appears that they (Satan and God) are co-conspirators in our suffering and adversity. Still, not all things appear as they really are.

I believe the key issue here is, again, the difference in the meanings of test and tempt but even more so, the intent and motive of the parties initiating the process itself, which would be God and the enemy of our souls.

God's intent and purpose in our hour of testing, whether in our loneliness, agony or misunderstanding, is to reveal our hearts and then change our hearts. God is about transforming us for good. As opposed to the devil, who is all about stealing, killing and destroying (John 10:10). God is not only our ally in the fight, but He is also the One who uses the tool to perform a distinct work or task and the tool that He often times wields is the devil himself.

> God has purposed in His grand design that we would rule and reign with Him. This process will require every instrument and tool in God's vast array of methods. The enemy's nature has been crafted by means of his own fall and rebellion. Yet he is one of many instruments or means God uses to forge the character of His saints (Isaiah 54:15-16).

The devil is not a co-worker with God or with us; he is our archenemy and a tool in the hand of God allowed to strike the piece of work and only at God's will and direction. The devil himself is harnessed to serve and perfect the masterpiece of God's design. The devil is no free agent running wild wreaking havoc on the saints.

Yes, he goes about as a roaring lion seeking whom he may devour, as the Bible clearly states, but for the child of God walking in obedience under the shadow of the Almighty he or she has nothing to fear. What comes down the pike has passed through the hands of our Father. In a fallen world, we constantly need to keep our eyes focused on God and remain tucked away in His presence.

Yes, God is in the picture and yes, "He causes all things to work together for good to those who love God, to those who are called according to His purpose" (Rom.8:28).

In our blunders, mistakes and even when we sin He is working it for good. He takes our self-willed, self-serving appetites and through time, fire and pressure, causes us to emerge victorious as we hold on to Him.

In times of our own obstinate rebellion and stiff neck attitudes God employs other means to bring us around. There is a **difference** between a genuine desire to love and serve God and just doing right religious things with no heart put into it, such as the 'traditional methods' or the children of Israel's 'ways', all of which have serious consequences.

Reminder: it is always about the heart. Get the intent right and the rest will follow.

Our place of departure is based on the intent of our heart and not a *fait accompli* or a finished work. An intent to obey God and walk in His ways is all He asks from us initially. What else do we have to offer Him or what else in all reality can we guarantee we will do for Him, nothing.

The devil is not an innocent bystander in this area of temptation. We may be drawn away of our own lust (and that is because we are not remaining hidden in Christ), but the character who knows us best, right after God, is the devil. Guess whose baited the lure with our own carnal man's favorite goodies and is trolling that lure right passed our noses! The fact that our enemy knows us so well should be of some concern to us.

He has been given a certain amount of leeway from God to wage his subversive war against us. You can be sure he has done his homework on all our idiosyncrasies. As fallen human beings on planet earth, we just happen to live in the war zone. There are no D.M.Z. (de-militarized zone) areas on the planet so it does matter where we run or try to hide from the warfare and temptations.

"No temptation has overtaken you but such as is common to man; and God is faithful, who will not allow you to be tempted beyond what you are able, but with the temptation will provide a way of escape also that you may be able to endure it" (1Corinthians10:13).

> The way of escape is not a deliverance from things but a way through them. To be delivered from our trials would contradict the latter part of the verse that says, "that we may endure it." We do not have to endure what we are free of.

Our view of scriptural promises is often influenced by our disdain of conflict and adversity. We pray and trust to be delivered from evil and that is only normal; who likes problems anyway? More often than not, every day brings its share of evil tidings as Jesus said "sufficient onto the day is the evil thereof" (Mathew 6:34).

However, the overcoming saint must be trained and taught to overcome more than just the TV remote control. In the war we will be tried and proven repeatedly; the fire of our trial will reveal the substance of our faith whether it be of gold or other precious metal and not wood, hay or stubble, which will be consumed (1 Corinthians 3:10-14).

How many of us have come to a place of feeling so overwhelmed and even hopeless in our trials and temptations? There are times when we just give in to our flesh and exclaim 'what's the use, this is stronger than I, why fight it, I know I can't win.'

We have all been down in that valley, where every fiber of our natural man desires to do what we knew was wrong but we felt we just could not go on one more minute without satisfying that desire or urge. We believed at the time there was no way to resist the flood of thoughts and emotions. Every part of us was desirous to satisfy our cravings even realizing before we did that we would be crying out to God in shame and repentance for having disobeyed and pursued our own lusts after the fact.

Oh, wretched man that I am, who will deliver me from my bondage. This is the 'Romans 7 cycle' of our fleshy desires. However, thank God for Romans 8.

Not only is there no condemnation to those who are in Christ Jesus, but the answer is that Christ took our place as sinful flesh as an offering for sin, therefore the requirements of the Law are fulfilled. We are free to walk away guilt-free.

The sons that are maturing are learning that their Father is graceful beyond imagination as they stumble along getting entangled and becoming un-entangled in their faith walks. In addition, we are not only becoming disgusted with our sin but our focus is shifting to pleasing God rather than our own flesh.

We are learning to submit first to God in order to better resist the enemy's attempts to lure us away to our former savory appetites. This will be our lifelong discipline but it can and will be done from the secret place of abiding and not resisting only.

> Disappointments, failure, and wounds from others seem to be breeding grounds that attract malicious characters. We need to be vigilant in our low times; the classroom in which we are receiving our eternal education looks more like a battlefield at times than a setting that's conducive to education.

"And Jesus full of the Holy Spirit, returned from the Jordan and was led about by the Spirit in the wilderness, for forty days, while being tempted by the devil…" (Luke 4: 1-2) The devil was not ignorant of who Jesus was; his strategy in this round of temptation would draw on all of his devious cunning and skill.

Remember it was the Holy Spirit that led Jesus into the wilderness to be tempted, not the devil. This was a divine setup. God led His Son into the wilderness to test Him and the devil, true to his nature, was perpetrating a minefield of temptation seeking to penetrate Jesus' protective shield and disqualify the Son of God.

We are not told what kind of temptation the devil used to try to lure the Son of God during those forty days. The Bible does however bear witness that at the end of those forty days the enemy came to Jesus and tempted Him again.

In Luke 4:3 we read, "And the devil said to Him, if you are the Son of God tell this stone to become bread." At a glance, this statement seems rather innocuous. For us this does not even register on our temptation meter. Do what? Is this supposed to be a temptation? We often tend to regard temptation as blatant, stark, in your face evil or obvious wrong. This was kind of a curve ball. At face value, it looks rather tame, but the devil had a big old hook hidden away in that lure.

The enemy's ploy was to move Jesus away from His place of abiding - just a slight deviation in the form of acting out on His own. Turning a few stones into bread is no big deal; He was hungry, right! The forty days were now over. What possible harm could it be? But the issue was not about bread, hunger or even timing; it was about absolute obedience. The devil knew he would never get Jesus to commit a blatant sin, but he might be able to tempt Jesus to move out independently of the Father and that would have constituted a sin. 'Jesus you have a legitimate need; you haven't eaten in forty days. Go ahead you deserve it. You went through forty hard days of fasting and praying; your Father won't mind, go ahead,' said the devil.

Waiting is never easy but it is necessary, and so Jesus waited for the provision of His Father - nothing else would do. Jesus could not have done it and remained the Lamb of God.

The second temptation: Jesus is given an offer the devil is hoping He cannot refuse.

We have to realize here that these temptations are not bogus or trivial in the sense that the devil had nothing that Jesus would have been interested in; otherwise, they are not temptations at all. Temptations are usually very relevant.

"All the kingdoms of the world have been given to me, I will give them to you if You will just bow down and worship me." Jesus was to inherit all the Kingdoms from His Father anyway but it would be by way of the cross, no shortcuts. This was the hook that 'did in' Adam and Eve. The devil has a high success rate in the way he awakens the passions and desires of our natural man, and in this case Adam and Eve began to question the goodness of God for them. God must be holding something good back from us; He did not tell us this side of the story. God does not want us to be like Him knowing good and evil and for good reason, which they only found out later. Again, the focus had to be, what did the Father want? Jesus' obedience to the revealed will and word of God was His hiding place.

The third temptation of trying to get Jesus to jump off the temple was to prove to everyone that indeed He was the Son of God. Everyone would see it and believe. The devil desired Jesus to move out on His own and accomplish His mission with a large center stage miraculous feat that would convince all that He was God and attract everyone to Himself, be accepted as the Messiah, and possibly change the course of history. This of course was the devil's hope that Jesus would buy into.

Did God tempt His Son? No, the Son was led into the wilderness to be tested to prove the character, worth and quality within Him. In that same wilderness, Satan was waiting to take advantage of the situation and try to persuade Jesus to act out on His own and forever abort our eternal salvation.

> So let us remember, temptation is a normal part of our lives as human beings on this planet. We will have to choose whom we will serve - God or our own self- interest. Our times of testing from the Father will be accompanied by His grace to be able to endure while being hammered by a devil trying to move us off our target of Christ-likeness. Submit to God first and then resist the devil, and he will flee.

Chapter 11

Honestly, Where Are We Going?

I sometimes get a little cynical with all the stuff that goes down in the Church. There seems to always be another wind blowing through and bringing with it strange new teachings with a checklist of "keys" to unlock spiritual truths with thirty ways on how to move in the power of God and these are different than the last thirty.

After a dozen or so teachings all with their own set of keys, it all starts to get a little fuzzy in the memory banks. No disrespect intended for the honest to goodness servants who study and aim to equip and feed their congregations well. Nevertheless, there is a nagging feeling inside that I am faced with: what am I really after; what am I reaching for?

> I really believe that it is the larger portion of the church body that sincerely desires God, His presence and His majesty. The church longs to see His power manifested in the earth and His Kingdom reign and authority established in the church and exercised in the world at large. It is not only our desire as individual members; it is also our prayer and our mandate from the Lord Himself (Mark16: 15- 20). The rule of God in the earth must be preceded by the rule of God in the hearts of true believers - true believers being the born again blood washed saints of God.

A large diversion in our modern day churches is our infatuation with entertainment. This may be due in part to the growing fast pace media making deep inroads into the church, and instead of rejecting it altogether we have opened the door and have been inundated by the force of this tsunami. It's just a whole lot easier to put the brain in park and enjoy our popular stars perform rather than deal with a Holy Ghost message that brings the searchlight of God uncomfortably close.

We've created our own celebrities not wanting to be outdone, trying to keep in step with our prime competitor, the world. We have opened up alternative avenues to reach people with the message but have we discerned the avenue runs both ways on the media highway. We send it out, but it is also an avenue that comes right back into the Church bringing with it a mixture of values, standards and a pluralism that continues to erode the faith, especially the faith of this younger generation, leaving them with an assortment of Christian world views.

Maybe it is a little simpler than all of the above; maybe it is more of a matter of boredom and we just need a whole lot more visual brain stimulation to keep us all awake on Wednesday nights and Sunday mornings.

'If Jesus were here He would use all the latest technology', were often told. Maybe, but I think He did rather well by word of mouth; all of Israel went out to Him. Is it really all about the success of getting out the message or the success of the messengers getting out their latest book or CD series? Is it not about motives, the heart and obedience?

There is also the Martha syndrome - the person hard at work in the labours of God. We all seem to be so preoccupied with so many good things; could we be suffering from a 'works mentality'? Unlike Martha who was waiting on the Lord hand and foot trying to serve up the gang a lunch, Mary had chosen the better part and that was sitting at the Master's feet and learning to rest and know the Lord's heart.

> We cannot apprehend for God or on His behalf until He has had some measure of apprehending or claiming the ground in us. Of course, there is the place for working and serving but not to the exclusion of forsaking the intimacy of our relationship with the Lord.

The hundred and one success books the world has authored have influenced the believer's mindset in no small way. We are the product of a generation of never enough and more is better. Envy is accepted as normal, almost as a good thing - a motivator to urge us on to higher and better. Competition is now a new fruit of the Spirit, is it not? Contentment is boring - a past tense attitude to have in a postmodern world where God's biggest prayer chore is to supply the high demands for more and more of everything that will make our lives easier and keep us satisfied lest we take our tantrums.

In our fast pace world God is allowed a certain window of time to answer prayer, otherwise we will just go out and buy it. He would not want us to go without too long; that would be a form of suffering, would it not?

Is it possible we have lost our ability to wait on God for however long until there is a breakthrough? What about our ability to hear His voice, and whose will determines the course of our lives anyway?

What about our money? This is a holy ground issue. God gets the ten percent and I get the ninety; that is fair. Let us not get too spiritual here and suggest that it is all God's anyway; that is a little over the top. I worked all week for it, and yes, I am thankful for the job, but God understands that I need more money in these trying economic times.

'My time' is another touchy subject that is also parceled out in very meager allotments. Remember it is a busy world so to be a well balanced steward, time is broken up so that everyone and of course God get some time with me and I get the balance to rest and have personal down time - a chance to recoup.

Honestly, what will God do with us? Have we really died? Have our lives been hidden with Christ in God? Are we seeking those things above more than the seeking of the earth (Colossians 3:1-2)?

Even as I write this section, I am very aware of my own personal 'heart condition'.

Three decades later, hundreds of books read and digested, sermons beyond number, meetings, powerful Holy Spirit encounters, hours without number in the presence of the Lord, and still I can somehow manage to lose my passion for God, become weary, get offended with the Church, people and at times even with God much to my shame and regret.

At time's I have been so low and discouraged I could not believe there was a way out or up from the pit I was in. Yet He remains forever faithful, true to His word and His promises. Just when I felt I could not take another step, my Father had a way to reveal Himself to me just to let me know He was there with me and to re-assure me by His gentle touch or a word that He was there and was committed to me no matter what.

> Stuff happens to every Christian. We live in a fallen world; we are going to go through, yes each one of us, some very dark nights of the soul. Our worlds are going to be turned upside down and everything is going to be shaken out of our pockets. We can rebuke the trials and adversities and command that they depart and be cast into the sea, but the chances are when we open our eyes they will still be there.

Our kingdoms and our rule over them must be abdicated; there can only be one true God in our universe; only One can rule and reign. He may have elevated us to be "seated in heavenly places with Him" but He still reserves His place as Lord and He demands to be obeyed and revered, not so much for His benefit but for ours.

If there is anything I have come to learn in my wildernesses, it is that though the giants in the land come out one after another,

I am still in the divine will of God nonetheless. In the financial pressures, at times a strained marital relationship, and health issues those giants were screaming at me, 'You're going down and you're not coming back up, it's over. Look at the mess you're in and it's all your fault' - which was not the truth, but in those moments that relentless pounding takes its toll and I begin to concede as I look at my circumstances and conclude God would not allow this unless I was guilty. At times, my thinking is off, I feel I missed the Lord somehow and now I am paying the penalty.

Before I concede any more ground to my enemy and sink deeper into his spiritual quicksand of lies and deception, let me state the following. If I walk with God on a day-to-day basis, in humility, with a surrendered heart and in obedience to the light that I have at the time, then I can rest assured that my acknowledgement of Him in all my ways has led me to this place. We need to take hold of this truth. We are in the center of His will if we are doing all we know to do, even if it seems the road is leading us to what resembles Hell itself (Proverbs 3:5-7).

When things turn upside down, and they often do, we may have no idea why. In our minds we have been faithful; we're walking the walk and trying to be as sensitive to God as we could. But this is the normal Christian walk. Remember Peter told us not to be surprised at the fiery trial that we all experience; it means we are on the right track no matter what our adversary is screaming into our ears.

One Saturday morning, I went out for breakfast with a friend. As good friends, we share a great deal about what is going on in our lives at the moment. This man has been in a very difficult place for many years and still is, for the most part, no fault of his own - life happens.

He related a few years back how he felt led to expand his personal business. He sensed the Lord direct him to move in that direction and so he purchased equipment and hired on more employees. Within a short time of implementing this business plan the economy went south and so did most of his business and he suffered a great loss. He has since had to sell the equipment at a substantial loss and layoff those employees.

As he is relating this story to me, which is ongoing, it is amazing how similar the parallels run with the events of my own personal life and business. We both love the Lord; we are both walking to the best of our ability in the light and will of God; we both prayed and sought God desiring His leading and open door, which in time we both felt happened, and so we went ahead with what we both believed to be the steps God was ordaining for us.

Twelve months later, the economy goes bust and so do the plans.

Now I know what some folks would say, 'well it probably wasn't God in the first place, or you just did not hear correctly or the timing was off or this or that because God won't allow His children to suffer such loss; He's a God of blessing and not of curses and this sounds like a curse to me.'

> Why is it that we automatically point to the devil when anything happens to us that in our opinion seems negative or bad? Is God only interested in our temporal ease and comfort? Is God's only desire for us our momentary happiness and security? The teaching on this continent has conditioned us to the idea that our God's focus is on the here and now of our well being; this is a tragic lie and misconception.

After all, God planned for Joseph to be thrown in prison: "until the time that his word came to pass, the word of the Lord tested him." God had to deposit in that future leader some iron in his soul and not just a whole lot of sugary cake. God's ultimate plan required a jail cell and a lengthy sentence for this future Prime Minister of Egypt (Psalms 105:16-20).

Look at verse 16: "He [God] called for a famine upon the land [not the devil]; He broke the whole staff of bread." It is no accident or fluke that we experience great difficulties; God put them in the script and we are not outside His will even if hell is breaking loose all around us. In fact God invites some hell to confront us at times to add more pressure to the equation making any human intervention ineffective.

We have to reject this wrong indoctrination. We can be blessed of God and still be fighting our way through some very dark seasons, and God like a loving Father, is cheering us on at the sidelines. The transforming of our minds in this area is critical. Without it, the enemy will keep pulling the same old mind games on us. Every time we find ourselves in difficulty we blame the devil or worst we think we've missed God and we start caving in under the devil's lying assault that we are stubborn and plowing ahead on our own steam disregarding the Holy Spirit's leading.

Being prayerful, seeking God and be willing to accept whatever our Heavenly Father decides is a good indicator that we are heading in the right direction and on the narrow road of His will. We need to stay the course of what we know God's word clearly reveals and to continue to follow the last set of God's personal instruction to us that line up with scripture.

What causes confusion are the ideas that have lodged themselves in our mind that God would not allow any harm to come our way (based on an isolated reading of certain scripture verses). This rings true to our natural, common sense.

> The variable here, however, is what we think is harmful from our natural, self-preservation instincts which are right and built in by God for the temporal. However, the temporal needs to give way to a greater truth with a higher perspective from an eternal standpoint. Being plunged by the perfect will of God into a jail cell like Paul and Silas or like Joseph opens up a dimension of worship, praise and intimacy beyond anything we may have known in our comfortable environment, although contrary to contemporary Christian teaching.

I would like to quote from the book <u>The Heavenly Man</u>. This story is about Brother Yun who came to be a powerful leader in the Chinese "House Church" movement that transformed and impacted China for Christ which is still happening today. This will certainly fly in the face of our North American theology when it comes to praying God's will or our own in those impossible situations.

> "Whenever I hear [Brother Yun speaking] a house church Christian has been imprisoned for Christ in China I don't advise people to pray for his or her release unless the Lord really clearly reveals we should pray that way.
>
> Before a chicken is hatched it is vital it is kept in the warm protection of the shell for 21 days. If you take the chick out of that environment one day too early, it will die. Similarly, ducks need to remain confined in their shell 28 days before they are hatched. If you take the duck out on the 27th day, it will die.
>
> There is always a purpose why God allows His children to go to prison. Perhaps it's so they can witness to the other prisoners, or perhaps God wants to develop more character in their lives. But if we use our own efforts to get them out of prison earlier than God intended , we can thwart His plans, and the believers may come out not as fully formed as God wanted them to be." (313, <u>The Heavenly Man</u>)

In our North American mindset, our mandate would have focused solely on the release or escape of that particular believer. Would we have questioned the fact that possibly the Lord had a greater purpose for that believer than just being released? God's greater purpose was to outfit that believer with more character and faith in jail than out, as well as impacting fellow prisoners or guards on the inside during their captivity which would bear fruit we never would have thought possible in such a place.

The Chinese Christians recognized an important truth that many times we have yet to learn over here in our countries. The lesson being that in every situation as believers, while we are doing the will of God we are never outside of His protection or purpose even if the circumstances appear to be contradictory to our natural finite minds.

We need to remember that to have a testimony will require we go through a test. To have a miracle will require that we be placed in impossible situations, and then God will do the miraculous.

That which does not make common sense or even defies it is the normal rule in the Kingdom. This is the place of deepwater, where our feet no longer touch the ground; things seem out of control, and we do not have a grip on our circumstances. It is a spiritual free fall with nothing to take hold of except God Himself. These are the higher ways He designs for us under His tutorage.

> The reality zone of the jail cell or the experience of being a captive in exile in a foreign land like Daniel and his friends opened the only possible doors for them to move into higher levels and dimensions of natural and spiritual influence. Not only for their lives but also to affect the futures of nations and peoples assigned under their care.

So before we get too critical of God's exceeding great and wonderful plans for us in those desert places we may now be living in for a season, let's refrain from the impulse that we know it all. Do we understand scripture so well that we can boldly state that God does not operate in such seemingly contrary ways to His word? The honest to God truth is that sometimes it takes very hard and painful things to shape our inner man to form the Godly character that reflects our risen Lord. The iron is best formed under the hammer only after being placed in the fiery furnace, only then it is put on the anvil to be hammered repeatedly by the choice tools of the Master Craftsman Himself.

What prevents us from embracing this truth is that same old fear. Can we really trust a God who would take His own children and dangle them over the fire to form them? What will He do to us if we give Him permission to do with us as He would? This is a little scary for some of us, is it not? He does what He wants, but He would rather that we willingly consent to His will.

Our fears paint a grim picture of God at times; we believe God will so afflict us and pour down such terrible hardships that we position ourselves to dislike Him or His methods before it happens. I think we try to scare God out of any thought of putting us through anything unpleasant. He is not out to make our lives religious, dry or unpleasant. It is not supposed to be some unbearable journey on this earth. I wonder where all those thoughts come from that paint God as some big, mean, distant, cold and insensitive character?

Of course, we all know people who have been through some of the worst things that life brings: the death of a child, divorce, abortion, terminal disease, sexual abuse, rape and the list of these horrendous things boggles the mind.

These moments are seared into our memory banks. The pain, the deep wounds, the continual replay in our minds is evidence of the gravity of the trauma. There is no way that we can simply apply a quick and easy band-aid answer. How can we make some kind of sense of the misfortunes of our lives and others when there is no logic or reasoning to explain the whys?

Like Job's friends who came to visit him, after hearing of the multiple tragic crises and upon seeing him covered in boils from head to toe, raised their voices and wept throwing dust over their heads. Then it says they sat down on the ground with him for seven days with no one speaking a word. They saw that his pain was very great (Job 2:12-13).

> Sometimes it is best to sit quietly and just be there when people are going through tragic moments. No amount of poetic words can soothe the aching heart while it grieves. We do not need to sound like Shakespeare or a Hallmark card.

It is better at times just to be close by. The time for words - sound words - will come when the person has had time to process things somewhat. God does take the brunt of our anger in these situations: that is O.K. He has wide shoulders and a tough skin;

He understands more than we could ever know. There are no pat answers but there are answers nevertheless.

Why does He allow tragic thing to happen? Why did He allow that to happen to me, to us? Why did He not step in and stop that from happening? How can God turn any of these tragedies around for good?

From our temporal place of viewing our lives, adversity is nothing but painful, uncomfortable and undesirable. That is why the events of our lives are not left up to our discretion. God in His exalted place has intricately considered our unique character and disposition and has ordained that certain things be allowed to shape us, much as a sculptor would handle a tool to form a work of beauty as he chisels away at the excess marble. What he envisions is the finished work that no one else can comprehend right now.

For the Christian man, woman or young person, our lives are not our own. What we surrendered to God He now lays claim to. Where He takes us and through whatever valley or mountaintop He may lead us through, we can rest in Him who has measured and considered every factor in the conforming processes of our lives: nothing has been overlooked.

Paul in his second letter to the Corinthian church wrote these words describing in part his travail and hardship in the work of the ministry: "Blessed be the God and Father of our Lord Jesus Christ, the Father of mercies and God of all comfort; Who comforts us in all our affliction so that we may be able to comfort those who are in any affliction with the comfort with which we ourselves are comforted by God" (2 Cor.1:3-4).

> Yes, God has purpose for even the most tragic events. We who are comforted by God in our afflictions will in time be able to comfort others with the comfort of God Himself. This is neither small nor insignificant.

A few verses later in 2 Corinthians 1:8, Paul continues: "For we do not want you to be unaware, brethren, of our affliction which came to us in Asia, that we were burdened excessively, beyond our strength, so that we despaired even of life; indeed, we had the sentence of death within ourselves in order that we should not trust in ourselves, but in God who raises the dead; who delivered us from so great a peril of death, and will deliver us, He on whom we have set our hope. And He will yet deliver us."

Paul experienced unimaginable atrocities against his person for the sake of the Gospel which were all foreordained of God. In Acts 9:16, God is telling Ananias that he needs to go and tell Paul the purpose God has for his life. Paul is a new disciple who is blind as a result of his conversion experience. Part of the message to Ananias in verse sixteen is "I will show him how much he must suffer for My name's sake." For a more detailed list of Paul's hardships and suffering, look at 2 Corinthians 11:23-29. For the sake of truth, we have to conclude with scripture that our God rules in the affairs of men - all of the affairs. In Christ we carry the hope that in all the events of our lives God is present and on His throne ruling and reigning.

However for the unbeliever (and we were all in that camp at one time as well), we were the children of disobedience - enemies of God. What right or privilege did we have in laying hold of God's promises? We were in a war zone, open targets for the enemy of our souls to afflict us because we were slaves in his kingdom. We wanted no part of God; we were just fine scratching out our existence in the darkness of our understanding.

How is it that we blame God so easily for the consequences of our own actions and sins? We were rebels, hostile towards God. Outside of God's favour and blessings, unlike the children of God, we were subject to the devil's assaults all the while being found on the other side of God's protective hedge.

God is not responsible for all the bad things that happen to people. Christians, sons and daughters, have a Father to call on in times of trouble. Even if the trouble comes from the hand of God, there is a place of rest and peace in the midst of the storm and the all-encompassing comfort of the Father in all our afflictions.

What athlete who wants to be a world champion does not push themselves to excruciating limits in training and exercise, disciplines in diet, work and rest to win, as Paul said, a perishable crown? Why then, will we not allow our Father to take us where He needs in order to place an imperishable crown on our heads? Have we given Him the reins of our lives? Can the devil get at us and do us harm outside of God's consenting to it?

Ponder this fictional example for a moment. Say I am talking to some real tough guy; he likes to go around and beat up on people. I know all about him, but because of his so call skill I want him to go out and fight my own son. I set the limits as to how far he can go; but within those limitations this thug has the freedom to exercise his muscle. My motive and desire for this altercation is that my son would be able to exercise his skill at not only resisting this thug but that he might be able to overcome his power.

In no way would I as a loving father put my son in a place where I thought he would be hurt or seriously beaten, but I initiated a confrontation that, left up to my son, would never have taken place. The confrontation was intended for my sons benefit. My son needed to know his opponents and his craft and likewise his own ability to fight to defend and subdue his rival.

God as a loving Father initiates these matches through our many trials in life. They are never meant to destroy but to equip His children to become more than they are at present. We can rest in the arms of Jesus and know that His eye is on the sparrow, and we are worth many sparrows.

> A crown will be placed on our heads one day, but today the treasure within needs to shine forth for all men to see. The value of that treasure is beyond price, and the cost of revealing the splendor of that treasure will require the breaking of our outward vessel through the multiple seasons of barrenness and trials.

Remember, gold is purified in the fire and steel is tested under great pressure. Whatever you are going through that may seem hard or even impossible, rest in the thought that, unless you are in rebellion against God, you are probably walking right in the center of His will. Though the purpose and reasons may not be clear, the fact that we are led into those places at all reveals that God is taking us into deeper places in Him.

The very fact that He leads us down those difficult roadways is proof that we have grown up in Him and are now able to take hold of His manifest grace in the tempest and to emerge on the other side still standing. Promotion is coming.

I write this sensing the confusion and grief many saints experience as they are led into the "Valley of the Shadow of Death", but remember He who leads us is also He who has gone before us. Only in Christ can we rest "for Thou art with me" (Ps.23:4). Remember, "even though [we] walk…" we will come through and goodness and mercy will follow us through and we will dwell in the house of the Lord forever.

There was a time when things both natural and spiritual were simpler and more contrasted. In today's world, it is like everything has come together like ingredients to a cake: a vast mixture of stuff that at one time could not be intermixed and blended together. Black and white, right and left - identifiable differences. That was then, but now so much is tangled and intertwined that it takes a good deal of fortitude to separate the many claims and ideologies begging to be heard and assimilated into the believer's heart. A return to some serious Bible study might be required to help us become more astute at discerning the real from the counterfeit.

> Where is the old rugged cross that generations of saints carried in obedience to Christ's command? Men and woman laid aside the world's lure of a life of self-interest and turned their backs on what many would call God's doorway to prosperity. They did not need ten confirmations; they knew certain roads led to a whole lot of mixture and compromise and wanted no part of it. They were content to do with less rather than gamble their spiritual fate away. Money is not evil nor should we despise the blessing of the Lord. But on the larger scale, we have moved far off the simple truth of God supplying only our needs and in its place we have a success-oriented, new, enlightened, church philosophy of everybody gets rich and nobody has to do without in this Promised Land of abundance.

An Outdated Gospel

It is a new age of being the masters of our own souls and destinies. We do not have to accept anything we do not like. We can change everything around us by speaking things into being; not necessarily by any leading of the Holy Spirit but only because we are annoyed at our own mundane, mediocre circumstances and we want some serious changes that will appease us and pacify us.

I thought this poem by Brenton Thoburn Hadley would remind us all of a past era in the Christian church where sacrifice, suffering and carrying the cross was the main staple of every preacher's sermons. It is called "The Nail-Pierced Hands":

> Lord, when I am weary with toiling,
> And burdensome seem Thy commands,
> If my load should lead to complaining,
> Lord show me Thy hands
> Thy cross torn hands,-
> My Savior, show me Thy hands.
>
> Christ, if ever my footsteps should falter,
> And I be prepared for retreat,
> If desert or thorn cause lamenting,
> Lord, show me Thy feet,-
> Thy bleeding feet,
> Thy nail-scarred feet,-
> My Jesus, show me Thy feet.
>
> O God, dare I show Thee
> My hands and my feet?

In closing this chapter, I put the following poem in as well to reinforce the idea of how saints of the past were not turned away by the teaching of the Cross, but embraced it.

> Hast thou no scar?
> No hidden scar on foot, or hand;
> I hear thee sung as mighty in the land,

I hear them hail thy bright ascendant star,
Hast thou no scar?

Hast thou no wound?
Yet I was wounded by the archers, spent,
Leaned Me against a tree to die; and rent
By ravening beasts that compassed Me, I swooned;
Hast thou no wound?

No wound? No scar?
Yet, as the Master shall the servant be,
And pierced are the feet that follow Me;
But thine are whole: can he have followed far
Who has no wound nor scar?

Amy Carmichael

Chapter 12

The Offense of the Cross

Enemies of the Cross

I have endeavored to state as accurately and as honestly as I know how the supreme importance of understanding the superlative wisdom of the Cross of Christ in the everyday life of the Christian. The teaching and preaching of the Cross in the North American church is as the setting sun in the West: a distant and fading natural phenomenon that has hit its zenith at high noon but at this time of the day is just about ready to disappear into the horizon, giving way to the night sky.

The Cross, just like the setting sun, begins its daily course through the heavens peering through the darkness in the early morning. As it makes its way across the sky, it attracts little or no attention as it slips out of sight and disappears.

> For those who have read this far, it's encouraging to know that there are still many who have rightly discerned an alarming attitude that has prevailed over the Western church in the last couple of decades. It is my prayer and I believe yours also, that we seek God for an awakening - a return to the God ordained, transforming powerhouse of the Cross to be heralded once again in the blood bought Christian church. There is a tide that needs to be turned to counter the prevailing emphasis of a self-gratifying Gospel that in its form is unable to bring the Body of Christ into the unity of the faith, the true knowledge of God, a mature man or woman into the fullness of Christ.
>
> Peter the apostle, describes Christians as aliens, strangers and pilgrims. We are not home yet. The earth, this world system is our mission field, not our long-term residence. We tend to forget that we are visiting with a purpose - a God ordained purpose.

It was stated earlier that as the Sons (we are all the sons of God as believers, just as we are all the Bride of Christ) in the same calling as the first born son, Jesus, we have come to do the will of the Father, period! There is no plan B to fall back on if plan A fails.

What is plan A? The conforming of the Sons into the image of God accomplished by way of our transforming road to our own Gethsemane and unto our own Calvary. Everything else is secondary in order of importance.

By sheer emphasis alone in New Testament scripture, we become aware of a constant repeated theme: the Cross replays and repeats itself in every book and in various ways. It is of no coincidence that the Holy Spirit personally dictated the key so desperately needed to bring about the abundant spiritual life of the believer and the secret for the overcoming saint of God in each generation.

In the following paragraphs, I would like to concentrate on the subject of losses. The meaning of the word loss in the dictionary is "the act or an instance of loosing possession, the harm or privation resulting from loss or separation." This state of being, this experience, is seldom mentioned in our testimonials; in fact it is a place in relation to how we are and not where we are: this place being the true essence of the health and vitality of our true spiritual condition.

Let me explain. In Philippians 3, starting with verse 7, Paul says, "But whatsoever things were gain to me, those things I have counted as loss for the sake of Christ." "Whatsoever things" are the earmarks of Paul's earlier success story before he knew Christ as his Savior. All of which were the pinnacle of his religion and culture. His story was the envy of his peers and the model to the nation.

In verses 5- 9, we read of Paul's gains:

"Circumcised the eighth day, of the nation of Israel, of the tribe of Benjamin, a Hebrew of Hebrews; as to the Law, a Pharisee. As to zeal a persecutor of the church; as to the righteousness which is in the Law, found blameless. But whatever things were 'gain' to me, those things I have counted as loss for the sake of Christ. More than that, I count all things to be loss in view of the surpassing value of knowing Christ Jesus my Lord, for whom I have suffered the loss of all things, and count them but rubbish in order that I may gain Christ, and may be found in Him, not having a righteousness of my own derived from the Law, but that which is through faith in Christ, the righteousness which comes from God on the basis of faith..."

Paul not only counted or esteemed those things as loss but all things to be loss to him.

The word loss in the Greek is the word *zemia* and it is used to describe loss as in the loss of a ship and its cargo. Paul is saying, 'all things that were of great personal gain to me and that elevated me to a position of prominence in the nation I now, since Christ has come in to my life, I count as loss; they are to be compared to a ship and all its cargo sunk.'

This can only be said in view of the surpassing value of knowing Christ Jesus as Lord. I would like to point out a vast difference - the difference between something which is taken and something which is given. This is not about losing something as if it were all taken from him in one fell swoop. That would still be difficult to count as loss; the difference being that with the latter one has no choice in the matter; it was just taken from out of our hands.

> Paul is emphasizing the 'counting'; there is thought involved in this decision. One must choose. Picture an accountant tabulating all the entries and coming to a final sum. Paul concluded after adding all the gain entries and seeing their total that in comparison to knowing Christ all these things amounted to a sunken ship and its cargo - a total loss not to be compared.

This, my friends, is the offense of the Cross - the loss. Our loss.

Loss never sits too well in the human heart; it has a tendency to begin to fester and develop into full-blown offense. Consider for a moment the general condition of people who attend church. One is not immune to offence even if one is part of a church fellowship. In fact, I believe we are more prone to be offended in the context of that environment, most of which, quite frankly, amounts to petty, silly things.

Because there are personal feelings involved, a door inside of us gets opened. Whether we feel slighted, rejected, overlooked, belittled, embarrassed or whatever, we take offence. Now this little offence is just not going to sit deep down there inside of us and be nice and quiet. It would be so much easier if we just took that offence to the foot of the Cross and left it there and moved on with our communion with the Body of Christ.

Where are the myriads of other fellow believers whose presence we have missed over the years who are no longer a part of the Church because they were offended, and now those of us still in the Church are part of a motley group labeled 'those Christians who hurt me' in very demeaning tones. Unable to resolve the issues, they are taken down by a comment, an innocent remark (or maybe not) from another believer never intending to hurt them in the first place or cause offence.

You may be wondering where I am going with this; please bear with me.

To concentrate on and analyze the subject of offence in the church is, in my opinion, missing the larger picture here however important it may be. Offences are part of just intermingling with other people; they happen.

Offence is personal; it touches us in the 'who we are' area – our core. Who I am is all of my sensibilities, my upbringing, my pride of life, civility, sense of decency, decorum, etiquette and so on. So being offended becomes a very big personal hit. And to clarify, not all offences are to be viewed as unreasonable or without merit; we can be offended by what someone intentionally says or does to us.

The point I'm trying to make is that offence deals with loss. As an example we may be offended with people if we feel we are not appreciated for who we are, and so we come away feeling a sense of loss: we feel a lack of respect shown to us.

For instance, our opinion at the last meeting was not even considered in the final decision on the colour of the church carpet. We tell ourselves it was not that they did not consider my opinion; it was the way they did it. 'I felt embarrassed in front of all those people; I felt belittled.' Again, we are dealing with a sense of loss. We get hurt; we get offended.

This is not aimed at the right and wrong of how we deal and treat each other. We are taught scripturally that we are to prefer and esteem others higher than ourselves, to lay down our lives for one another (Philippians 2:2-5). The reality is, we fail to achieve this goal for whatever reason and people are hurt.

God in His sovereign way places us altogether in a group called the church. The Greek word is *ekklesia* made up of two words: *ek* which means "out of" and *kaleo* which means "to call" - our word for assembly or church. We have been 'called to Christ and called out of the world.'

> So many backgrounds, so many cultures - what a place to grow! All of us rubbing shoulders at meetings and gatherings just being ourselves; many times oblivious to the person next to us who is taken back by our 'backwoods demeanor' as we dig into the bowl of chips with our bare hands and we are left wondering why they gasp in astonishment.

So how do we deal with the area of personal offence? Paul states, "he has counted all things to be loss..."; let's look again at the dictionary meaning of loss.

Loss: "The act or instance of loosing possession, the harm or privation resulting from loss or separation." Loss means losing possession for a moment, an instance or forever. Loss brings with it harm and privation or being deprived, as in lacking the necessities of life.

Paul's gains listed in Philippians 3 amounted to what we would consider every facet of one's life: his race, culture, family, heritage, upbringing, education, career, service, profession, ministry, employment, creed and personal belief.

His life was a life where all the T's were crossed and all the I's were dotted. Refined, professional, dignified, respected and politically correct in every sense of the word: He was the who's who in the Jerusalem tabloids.

However, how do these gains stack up in the Kingdom? They do not! Of course, we are to give honour to whom honour is due and show respect; this is not about marginalizing Godly wisdom and some common sense.

Paul counted them all to be loss in view of the surpassing value of knowing Christ Jesus as Lord, but I would venture to say that he counted them to be loss also because they were manmade walls that divided the various people groups God wanted him to reach.

> God had to deal with Paul in the 'gains' department so that the enemy would not be able to sideline Paul as he was sent across every imaginable physical, emotional, social and political barrier that existed in his day: Romans, barbarians, idol worshippers, sick and diseased individuals, slaves, prisoners, blasphemers, brutes, gruff, ignorant, primitive and the whole gamut of the human condition all sitting in darkness, bound up in spiritual chains waiting to hear the Good News. What had formed Paul had to be renounced! God had to remake Paul so that the great apostle would not fall prey to the offence weapon and be taken out of the picture.

Oh, that we would become all things to all men (1 Corinthians 9:19)! How our sensibilities and refinements become the enemies' target for our taking offence and nursing our wounds as we pull away from the very place God has placed in our lives to overcome these barriers - the Church. The magnitude of offended, 'stay at home' Christians is off the charts!

Think of it: a mighty army sidelined for a lack of boots; it would not make any sense. The war is raging and this part of the army is sitting by, unable to join the conflict for lack of footwear. Quite frankly it's ridiculous! Look around, how can this mighty army of God, designed to war against the forces of darkness, be reduced by such petty rivalry?

The offence of the Cross encompasses more than the heavy duty suffering and adversity that comes knocking on our door at times. Yes there are times when we feel as Paul did in 2 Corinthians 1:8: "For we do not want you to be unaware, brethren, of our affliction which came to us in Asia, that we were burdened excessively, beyond our strength, so that we despaired of life." We have all had our moments of being overwhelmed by the suffering or adversity before us.

The offence of the Cross has also anticipated "the little foxes that spoil the vines": the slights, being overlooked, not being asked to be part of this team or that team, not used enough, used too much, cut in line, lunch was late.... All of these so called incidents are part of the similar testing that goes into proving the character of the man or woman of God. The boulders in the road are obvious; it's the smaller stones that twist our ankles and bring harm to our feet thus impeding our walks.

God's desire to pattern us after Jesus or even Paul so often gets ditched because we have not counted all things to be loss; the surpassing value of Christ Jesus as Lord remains in the 'theory' part of our divine instructions. We continue to embrace our earthly, natural character formation rather than taking hold of the heavenly pattern of death to self, denying self, esteeming others more important than ourselves; we are still so very much alive in our natural man.

> The little foxes are the little offences that in time spoil our connection to the Vine - Jesus Himself - and blemish any fruit that was developing. These little foxes should be a welcome harbinger: a signal of how much more needs to be counted loss, how much more needs to die, so that much more of His life can be imparted.

Paul not only counted them to be loss, but also as rubbish, even dung as some versions render verse 8. Now, this gets a little more serious as we look at verse 18 in the same chapter. Paul goes on to talk about knowing Him, and the power of His resurrection, and the fellowship of His sufferings. He continues with the call to press on to lay hold of that for which God laid hold of him. Press towards the prize Paul affirms, and then he brings up a few interesting points.

In verse 15 he teaches, "Let us therefore, as many as are perfect, have this attitude; and if in anything you have a different attitude, God will reveal that also to you...." Let's keep this all in context. As many as are perfect, mature, grown and complete have this attitude.

What attitude? The attitude found in the previous verses dealing with loss and pressing ahead. Then, if anyone has a different attitude, God will show you. God will reveal where we are coming up short, where we are still bound up or holding on to things we should not, our desire to hold on to former things.

Now tie this in with what follows in verse 17: "Brethren, join in following my example, and observe those who walk according to the pattern you have in us." It is quite clear that Paul is saying 'what you see in me (Paul) and in my life - this is the pattern; walk in it.' How many of us could say that? Yet he said to observe those who did. On the flip side of this pattern is where I've been trying to get to as we come to verse 18 and 19.

If there ever was a more sobering warning in the New Testament this one would certainly be on the same level of importance in regards to heeding the teaching of chapter 3 of Philippians. Verse 18-19: "For many walk, of whom I often told you, and now tell you even weeping that they are enemies of the cross of Christ, whose end is destruction, whose god is their appetite, and whose glory is their shame, who set their minds on earthly things."

These people who were once believers are now enemies, adversaries or hostile towards the cross - the cross being the place of death, denying of self and exposure to death. In their minds they may still love God and Jesus but towards the cross and its demand that we should all die and count all to be loss - even all that has formed us - they are now hostile. The cross is no longer allowed to be applied to them; they have rejected the pattern, the example, the die casting to be made identical, not to Paul, but to Christ.

Please hear me. Paul the apostle wrote this, not me. "Whose end is destruction": this is a heavy-duty warning for all of us. When we refuse to allow the Holy Spirit to deal with us and we no longer allow the cross to execute our carnal, fleshy, self-made ideals, opinions and attitudes we have moved into the realm of being hostile towards the Cross of Christ.

"Whose god is their appetite…who set their minds on earthly things." The word appetite could be rendered belly, cavity, womb or the heart. These people are ruled by their own heart. Out of the abundance of their own heart come, the very things they have set their minds on which in this case are the things of the world taking precedence over the things of God. Their own appetites rule them. A good indicator that the cross is offensive and has been laid aside in our lives is an increased desire and interest in worldly trends. A shift in our passion for Christ, a business and preoccupation with natural things.

Another reference is found in 2 Timothy 4:10: "for Demas [a former co worker with Paul, Philemon verse 24] having loved this present world has deserted me and gone to Thessalonica;" These were not isolated cases; Paul says in Philippians 3:18 that "many walk..." which are now enemies of the Cross.

Remember the children of Israel perished only because God could not take them any further. They grumbled, complained and accused God of wanting to kill them in the wilderness. God could not remove Egypt from their hearts even though God had removed them from Egypt.

We absolutely need to embrace Paul's example to come into a mature and complete man by renouncing the things that have formed us that are contrary to Godliness and righteousness, to count them all to be loss, of no value, as a sunken ship and its cargo. We cannot allow petty insignificant offences to sideline us from coming into the calling and purpose for our lives and to bear much fruit.

> We must resist every inclination to take offence; this is a key strategy of the devil to divest the saints of their inheritance in Christ by pushing them to be hostile towards the disciplines of the Father by way of His Cross.

The new man in Christ must be willing to cross denominational lines to speak for Christ; he or she must be willing to cross the street to touch people of different cultures and backgrounds, whether brutish, rough or ignorant individuals. We must be willing to obey God when our feelings are hurt and we want to pull back and accuse leadership of preferring others and not recognizing our gifts and talents. Our subsequent inclination to stay home alone and be spiritual on our own is not the New Testament pattern.

Resurrection life is only possible after the death of the sons. Today, we all need to take a close look at what offends us. Our humanity is being broken down piece by piece and Christ is being formed in us piece by piece. We all get hurt; it just happens. Most of what offends us is unintentional, done by people who most often have no idea what they have done. What offences reveal in us, about us, is worth taking to the Cross. We cannot afford to let offence produce a spiritual cancer in us.

Let us press on and lay hold of what Christ has for us, let us suffer the loss of everything that has formed us into a different image other than that of the Son of God. We must embrace the tearing down of the natural man who stands in the way of our completeness in Christ.

"Seeing that His divine power has granted to us everything pertaining to life and godliness, through the true knowledge of Him who has called us by His own glory and excellence. For by these He has granted to us His precious and magnificent promises, in order that by them you might become partakers of the divine nature, having escaped the corruption that is in the world by lust" (2 Peter 1: 3-4).

Wilbur Chapman looked into the rugged face of General Booth (Salvation Army) one day and asked, What is the secret of your power and success? Tears stole down his cheek. Then brushing back the hair on his brow, furrowed through the years of battles, trials and victories, he said, "I will tell you the secret. God has had all of me there was to have. There have been men of greater opportunity, but from the day I caught a vision of what Jesus Christ could do, I gave all to Him." (The Cross and Sanctification page 184)

Chapter 13

Gethsemane

In this last chapter, I cannot get away from the thought of the Garden of Gethsemane. It sounds like a nice place. This was a garden on the Mount of Olives familiar to Jesus and his disciples. More than likely, it was a place they visited frequently - a getaway kind of place away from the crowds, the noise, the demands and the needs. It was a place to be alone.

It is here, at a very crucial time and place, and with a particular purpose, that Jesus came. There was still one matter that needed to be addressed. This night would be a long night. With sleepy disciples in tow, Jesus left them asking them to pray and stay alert, which was the last thing on their minds after such a grand Passover meal. Nothing was more appealing at this point than a little shut-eye. They were oblivious to what was at hand.

What had been long foretold, what He had been sent for, and what He had willingly chosen to do - the cup - was to be taken completely in hand and drunk.

No man had ever sensed such oppression as all of Hell was converging on the Son of God in an attempt to overwhelm Him with despair, fear and hopelessness. Soon the mob would move in, led by a friend who betrayed Him for a few silver coins.

> What he would endure in these next hours is beyond description as it extends beyond the realm of natural men driven by an unquenchable thirst for blood, violence and murder demonically stimulated - the imaginations of men further heightened by malevolent entities ever raising the malicious bar of cruel strategies to assault the Rabbi of Israel.

Compare truth, purity, righteousness, grace and mercy in human form in contrast to the devilish assaults verbal, physical and yes, spiritual through the mouth and hands of unredeemed men. Fallen beings angry, hateful, accusing, lying, hitting, slapping, spitting, punching, humiliating and shaming the Son of Man: the final hours of His suffering were now at hand.

"Father, if Thou art willing, remove this cup from Me; yet not My will, but Thine be done" (Luke 22:42). 'I know what lies ahead of Me Father; I don't want to have to go through this; I don't know if I can. Please take this cup away from Me so that I don't have to endure this suffering."

This was the unsettled business; Jesus was pleading 'take it away from Me; I don't want to do this.' We forget the humanity of Jesus at times. He knew what He was in for: betrayed by friends, forsaken by friends, denounced by friends, tortured and crucified for those same friends and yes all the rest of us. Isolated and alone He had to face the looming onslaught.

> Gethsemane means the "oil press". Here in a garden where olives were harvested and pressed for their oil, Jesus was undergoing the press of a different kind. The final signature at the bottom of the contract was being inscribed with His blood and sweat as He wrestled with the forces of Hell itself that were inciting every cell of His natural life to rise up, throw off the yoke of conformity to the Father and insert His own will. He had a body, emotions, passions, feelings and a separate will. Up until now He had never questioned the Father.

Jesus' will and His volition became the target of satanic influence bearing down on this silhouette kneeling in the darkness of Gethsemane.

We know ourselves how difficult it can be to let go. We have no assurance but God's word that there is something on the other side better than what I now hold in my hand. Faith, trust, why must it always come down to this.

We cannot see or know by our senses what God asks of us many times. We wrestle with our feelings, our thoughts and other entities that have crept into our Garden unaware in order to further make the right choice either impossible or in the very least extremely complex.

Gethsemane, as difficult a place as it is, is absolutely necessary. Jesus could not have gone to the cross and accomplished the Father's purpose had He gone there from the Last Supper. Closure was needed - in fact absolutely indispensible.

As Jesus faced His final hours and the reality of the moment began to flood His being, one thing remained. Everything in eternity for man hinged on this one last decision; everything about Jesus also hinged on this one final choice.

> The death of Jesus and everything else that would subsequently follow happened in Gethsemane. The colossal struggle that ensued in the darkness was settled after one man looked beyond the fallen players in this horrific real life drama and for the last time on this earth gazed into the eyes of His beloved Father as the Lamb without spot or blemish and with simple trust surrendered His last and only objection.

In a moment, He would become sin. He who knew no sin became the embodiment of sin and thus He was separated from the lifeline of love and fellowship He had ever known in all eternity. It was gone, for now.

With His last moments of earthly life only hours away, here in this Garden, Jesus acquiesced spirit, soul and body into the Father's hands. One will, one choice, one act of obedience would forever secure our salvation wrought in the resolute heart of the Christ. The Son of God was now perfected.

"In the days of His flesh, when He offered up both prayers and supplications with loud crying and tears to Him who was able to save Him from death, and who was heard because of His piety, although He was a Son, He learned obedience from the things He suffered; and having been made perfect, He became to all those who obey Him the source of eternal salvation" (Hebrews 5:7-9).

If it were not for Gethsemane, could He have faced the angry mob? Would He have turned the other cheek as they slapped, spit and struck the Son of God mercilessly, all the lies and the accusations taking their toll? Could He have said in that Garden, as Peter tried so valiantly to defend His Master, 'put away your swords, don't you realize that I could call at this moment twelve legions of angels to deliver Me... (My rendering. Matthew 26:52-53)

God help us in our hour of great testing if we have not been in Gethsemane! We may have already surprised ourselves to how low we can squirm when Hell is unleashed in our face. The Son of God found an altar in that Garden where He laid the last vestige of His will and offered it all up to the Father. With the final renunciation of self settled, what remained now was the wooden stake.

He could now leave the Garden secure, encased in the knowledge that He was heard and, now for the joy set before Him on the other side of His crucifixion, He would endure the Cross. How we must visit and allow Gethsemane to do the work of the press.

> How often we struggle through our dark night of the soul; we emerge many times not having been pressed out of the hard shells that encapsulate our hearts. We are not ready to meet the mobs, the anger and the insensitivity of the world or for that matter, other believers. We are easily moved away from our spiritual hiding place in Christ and are pulled into conflicts and situations we have not prepared for. There are no angels to call on, only our putrid flesh.

There is a Garden before or in every wilderness, adversity, or Cross. How we resist and fight to bypass this wonderful place of exchange. With difficulty, we surrender our rights and sense of justice to God who seems all too often indifferent to our plight. Deep down I know all too well His ways are true and right and the grace to face the real life drama unfolding around me awaits my capitulation.

The Holy Spirit bids us to tarry here; the Father waits to gaze into our eyes, to reassure us that we will get through our dark night. Just one look into the Master's eyes invites us to surrender the last remnant of our own right to choose our outcome. We cannot help but yield in complete trust, and in that very moment, His grace is fused to our soul.

> We will emerge from Gethsemane's winepress enabled to pick up our Cross and carry it to its appointed place of death. We will rise from this place having known the fellowship of His sufferings and now the power of His resurrection.

Nevertheless, not my will, but Thy be done.

In closing I make an appeal to every saint whose heart is stirred with passion for Jesus Christ. There are no shortcuts or magic wands that transform us in an instant. Our calling and the way before us is made sure by Him who has gone before us. Our path is riddled with countless obstacles meant to harm and even destroy our relationship with God.

Many of us have learnt to some degree our inability to do anything of eternal value in and of ourselves; we have come away from our ordeals with God with a limp, as Jacob did. This 'limp' is our reminder of our great big God who has calculated the smallest details that at times so easily overwhelm us and has made provision for us. We are not used to being laid low or humbled in fact most of us detest it greatly. However the Spirit of God bids us to take the form of a bondservant as Jesus did .With this mindset we need to begin to serve where we are not for anything more than just learning to obey some very basic Kingdom principles that open doors in God's due season of time.

This open door will not likely be a promotion but rather an entrance into His Presence, not earned but freely given to those favored whose hearts have come under the yoke of His obedience and have surrendered their shoulders to His harness.

At this juncture we will finally begin to realize the reward of those who like Jesus express with the upmost fervor "I have come to do Thy will O My God, Thy laws are written in my heart." Secure and at rest in ways and purposes far beyond my abilities to understand, Gethsemane no longer poses a threat to me, Gethsemane, has become the place of my deepest communion with My Father and the source of abundant life.

Author Biography

Rene Caza lives in Kingsville Ontario Canada. He has spent ten years in Men's Jail Ministry. He teaches Christian foundation classes and is currently involved with Men's ministry in his local church. Rene is married to his wife Yvonne they have three children and three grandchildren.

rene@canadianplumbline.com
www.canadianplumbline.com

LaVergne, TN USA
25 January 2011
213764LV00002B/2/P